Masterbuilt Electric Turkey Fryer Cookbook for Beginners

Amazingly Easy Recipes to Fry Turkey, Boil Seafood, Steam Vegetables, and More

Kinze Dous

Table of Contents

Introduction

Turkey is one of the most favorite dishes of an American tradition most of the people like to serve turkey for celebrating a special occasion like Christmas and weekend parties. Cooking turkey with traditional method using oven may be a challenging and time-consuming method. One of the leading turkey fryer manufacturers Masterbuilt makes a unique and advanced electric turkey fryer kitchen gadget which helps you to prepare your favorite bird within very less time at home.

The Masterbuilt electric turkey fryer is made up of stainless steel body and comes with detachable heating elements and a control panel. It is one of the versatile cooking appliances used as a fryer, steamer, or boiler. Its large cooking basket is capable to hold up to 20 lb of turkey at a time. The fryer comes with various features like overheat protection, adjustable temperature setting knob, non-stick interior, built-in drain valve for easy cleaning, and more. The Masterbuilt electric turkey fryer uses 33 % less oil compared to the other traditional fryer.

The book contains 100 different types of recipes like poultry, pork, beef & lamb, fish& seafood, vegetarian and side dishes. All the recipes written in this cookbook are unique and written in an easily understandable form. The recipes are written with their perfect preparation and cooking time with step by step cooking instructions. Finally, all the recipes end with their nutritional information. The nutritional value information helps you to keep track of daily calorie consumption and also helps you to determine that you have taken a healthy and nutritious meal. There is less book available in the market on this topic thanks to choosing my cookbook. I hope you love and enjoy all the recipes written in this book.

Chapter 1: Masterbuilt Electric Turkey Fryer Basics

If you are one of those who love deep-fried turkey and want to enjoy your holiday by serving crispy golden brown turkey which is tender and juicy flesh from inside. Then the Masterbuilt electric turkey fryer is one of the best indoor electric deep fry having the capacity to fry the whole turkey. The Masterbuilt electric turkey fryer comes in 20 lb cooking capacity and is made up of high-quality stainless steel material. It is a multifunctional cooking appliance which not only deep-fries your food but also steams and boils your favorite food.

The Masterbuilt electric turkey fryer requires less oil as compared to other models of a turkey fryer. It comes with lots of features which make your cooking process easy like a thermostat, built-in timer, orange led light which illuminates when the power supply is on and green light illuminates when the inside cooking oil temperature reaches its set temperature position to begin cooking process.

The Masterbuilt electric turkey fryer is loaded with advanced security features which ensures your safety while you are cooking. It is loaded with auto shut-off security feature which ensures that when the temperature goes on high the appliance is automatically shut down. A lifting hook will help you to remove the turkey safely from the hot oil basin and also help to keep the food basket safely in place. The fryer comes with two oil fill line one is for a minimum amount of oil to full-fill the first oil level mark. It requires 1.5 gallons of oil for minimum level and for maximum level mark it requires 2.75 gallons of oil. Always keep in mind t6hat do not overfill the oil above its recommended level. The timer dial is present at the control panel to adjust the desired temperature as per recipe needs. Using this dealer you can adjust the temperature settings up to 375°F.

Easy cleaning process adds one more advantage while using this appliance. If you want to remove the cooled oil from the Masterbuilt fryer it comes with a drain valve to remove the oil from fryer. It also has removable spout attachment which helps to drain the hot oil safely. If you are finding the alternative for roasting and want to cook delicious dishes indoor. Then Masterbuilt electric turkey fryer is one of the best options available in the market.

Features of Masterbuilt Electric Turkey Fryer

- Best Indore Turkey Fryer

The electric Masterbuilt turkey fryer is one of the handy and convenient turkey fryers specially design for indoor use. It is the best option for those people who don't have an outdoor cooking space but want to enjoy their weekend with deep-fried turkey. The appliance is handy and you can easily carry it for indoor and outdoor use even you can use it in your garage. It fry, boil, and steam your favorite food easily, it takes less than 2 hours to fry the whole turkey and gives you constant delicious fried results.

- Huge Cooking Capacity

The Masterbuilt turkey fryer comes with a huge 20 lb of cooking capacity at once. It is one of the best choices for those people who want to enjoy fried food at a weekend party. You just need to put the bird under 20 lb on its back into the frying basket and put it into the electric fryer. The single deep-fried turkey is enough to feed 11 to 14 peoples at a time.

- Adjustable Temperature settings

The Masterbuilt turkey fryer comes with adjustable temperature settings knob. You can adjust the temperature settings between 125 °F to 375 °F. You can cook a wide variety of delicious dishes using this variable temperature setting modes. The green light ignites when the inside temperature of the oil reaches its set limit. You never need to check the temperature by using a thermometer.

- Versatile deep fryer

The Masterbuilt fryer is one of the versatile cooking appliances not only use to deep fry but also used to steam and boil your favorite foods. You can fry your favourite chicken, turkey, fish, French fries and also boil or steam seafood's like lobsters, crabs etc. While frying food you can use oil and boiling or steaming purpose you can use water.

- Safe to use

The Masterbuilt fryer is one of the safest cooking appliances comes with an auto shut off option. When the fryer inner temperature goes hotter than desire temperature it shut down automatically. The fryer equipped with thermostat device which automatically senses and control the inner temperature of the turkey fryer. It also comes with two light indicator orange and green. The orange light indicates the power supply is on and green light indicates the oil is heated enough or ready to start cooking. The fryer has minimum and maximum oil level marks which ensure you to maintain the correct level of oil. Don't overfill the pot above the maximum level mark.

- Easy to clean

The easily removable inner pot makes your cleaning process easy. You just need to pull up the inner pot from the main unit and clean it into the dishwasher. The Masterbuilt fryer also equipped with a drain valve which helps to remove the oil easily from the fryer to start the cleaning process. The removable parts like inner pot, food basket, drain valve, and pot lid are dishwasher safe so you can easily clean it into the dishwasher.

How to Use Your Masterbuilt Electric Turkey Fryer?

The master electric turkey fryer is easy to use by following the instructions given below.

1. First, mount the side control panel and heating elements at a down position on the mounting bracket. The heating element position inside the fryer pot will ensure that the control panel is attached its right position. Make sure the heating elements are fully immersed in oil or water during first use.
2. If you want to steam or boil your food then fill the minimum level 1.5 gallon or maximum 2.75 gallons of water. If you want to deep fry your food then always fill the pot at the maximum level (2.75 gallons).
3. Plug the power cord to the control panel. Make sure "This side up" message is shown on the top will ensure the proper power connection.
4. Power on the main switch. If the orange light turns ON, it means that the heating elements and control panel mounted its right position in the bracket.

5. Turn the round dial to set the desired temperature as per your recipe needs. When the green light will turn ON then it indicates that the appliance has reached its desire temperature and it is ready for use.

6. When the cooking time is finished then unplugs then unplugged the power cord and opens the lid of the fryer. Use the double lifting hook to remove the food basket safely from the main unit.

7. When the oil is cool down then use the drain valve to remove the oil from fryer.

How to Operate?

- Steam

Add water into the fryer at its maximum line mark (2.75 gallons).

Make sure the water level doesn't cross the max line mark.

Always keep watch on water level if the water evaporates completely it may overheat the appliance.

While using steaming or boiling cooking method set the temperature dial at 375 °F to ensure the fryer will not cycle and the water boiling continuously.

- Drain valve

Always make sure that drain valve is set OFF position until the cooking process not finish.

To drain the liquid from the pot first remove the safety cap from the drain valve.

Then screw the valve spout on the drain valve carefully.

Always remember that do not over tighten the valve spout to drain valve. This may damage the valve thread and cause the leakage.

Then set the spout into the right position in which the opening is facing down position. Then open the drain valve to drain out liquid from the pot.

When the pot is empty then close the drain valve. Keep in mind that do not store the water into the fryer.

- Reset Appliance

Your Masterbuilt electric fryer comes with overheat protection safety feature.

When the appliance is overheating then it automatically shuts off.

You need to reset the appliance at this stage. First, unplug the appliance and remove the control panel.

From the inner side of the control panel, there is a hole. Insert the toothpick into a small hole of the control panel to push the button.

This will help you to reset the appliance.

- Cavities

The cavities area of the appliance is present in three corners and design to catch the grease and condensation created due to steam.

After every use doesn't forget to wipe out the cavities with the help of a damp cloth.

While steaming process cavities are full before finishing the cooking. Drain it with the help of absorbent material like a sponge.

- Cleaning and Maintenance

Before starting the cleaning process unplugs the appliance from the power socket. Let it cool down for 2 hours if there is water and 5 hours when using oil.

Always clean your Masterbuilt electric turkey fryer after every use.

Clean the inner pot, food basket, lid, lifting hook and valve spout with the help of damp cloth or soapy water. You can also clean it into the dishwasher because all these parts are dishwasher safe.

Clean heating element, outer body and control panel with the help of clean damp cloth or sponge. Do not put these parts into the dishwasher because they are not dishwasher safe.

Dry all these parts thoroughly before assemble it.

FAQs

- Why the fryer won't turn ON?

This is happening due to incorrect control panel mounting. The control panel comes with a safety switch which must mount properly over mounting bracket given outer side of the pot. When the orange light illuminates it indicates that the control panel mounted properly.

- Which is the best oil used in the fryer?

You can use any type of oil into fryer but it is recommended that use peanut oil due to its higher smoke point and its great taste.

- How much oil require in the fryer?

To fill the maximum level mark your fryer requires 2.75 gallons of oil. It is recommended that when you are frying your food the oil must be filled up to its maximum level mark.

- How to reset the appliance?

When the appliance is overheating then it will shut off automatically. To reset it again you have to need a toothpick to insert into the small hole to push the reset button present on the control panel. Using this method you can easily reset your appliance.

- What kind of temperature settings is given?

The temperature settings are given from the range minimum 125°F to a maximum of 375 °F. You can set the temperature in between giving range as per your recipe needs.

Chapter 2: Poultry

Easy Fried Chicken Wings

Preparation Time: 10 minutes
Cooking Time: 12 minutes
Serve: 6

Ingredients:

- 2 lbs chicken wings
- ¼ tsp cayenne
- 1 tsp garlic powder
- 1 cup soy sauce
- 1 tsp ground black pepper

Directions:

1. Add chicken wings and soy sauce to the mixing bowl. Cover and set aside for 1 hour. Drain well and pat dry chicken wings with paper towels.
2. Preheat the peanut oil to 375 F in electric fryer.
3. Add chicken wings in basket and fry in hot oil for 12 minutes. Drain on paper towels.
4. Add fried chicken wings to the mixing bowl. Add cayenne, garlic powder, and black pepper over chicken wings and toss well.
5. Serve and enjoy.

Nutritional Value (Amount per Serving):

- Calories 313
- Fat 11.2 g
- Carbohydrates 3.9 g
- Sugar 0.8 g
- Protein 46.5 g
- Cholesterol 135 mg

Crispiest Chicken Tenders

Preparation Time: 10 minutes
Cooking Time: 6 minutes
Serve: 8

Ingredients:

- 8 chicken tenders
- 1 egg, lightly beaten
- 6 tbsp milk
- 6 tbsp dill pickle juice
- 1 tsp paprika
- 1 tsp garlic powder
- 6 tbsp flour
- 6 tbsp cornstarch
- 1/8 tsp cayenne
- ¾ tsp seasoning salt

Directions:

1. Add egg, milk, and dill pickle juice in a large bowl and mix well. Add chicken tenders in bowl and coat well, cover, and place the bowl in the refrigerator for 30 minutes.
2. Add cornstarch, flour, garlic powder, paprika, cayenne, and seasoning salt in a large zip-lock bag and mix well. Add chicken tenders in bag, seal bag, and shake to coat chicken tenders.
3. Preheat the peanut oil to 375 F in electric fryer.
4. Add coated chicken tenders in the basket and fry in hot oil for 6 minutes or until golden brown. Drain on paper towels.
5. Serve and enjoy.

Nutritional Value (Amount per Serving):

- Calories 323
- Fat 16.6 g
- Carbohydrates 26 g
- Sugar 1.1 g
- Protein 16.5 g
- Cholesterol 62 mg

Coconut Chicken Tenders

Preparation Time: 10 minutes
Cooking Time: 6 minutes
Serve: 4

Ingredients:

- 1 lb chicken breasts, cut into strips
- 2/3 cup breadcrumbs
- 2/3 cup shredded coconut flakes
- 2 tbsp milk
- 2 eggs, lightly beaten
- ½ tsp chili powder
- ½ cup flour
- ¼ tsp pepper
- ½ tsp salt

Directions:

1. In a shallow bowl, mix flour, pepper, chili powder, and salt.
2. In a separate shallow bowl, whisk eggs with milk.
3. In a shallow dish, mix coconut flakes and breadcrumbs.
4. Toss chicken tenders in flour mixture then dip in the egg mixture and coat with coconut flakes mixture.
5. Preheat the peanut oil to 375 F in electric fryer.
6. Add coated chicken in a basket and fry in hot oil for 6 minutes or until golden brown. Drain on paper towels.
7. Serve and enjoy.

Nutritional Value (Amount per Serving):

- Calories 427
- Fat 16.4 g
- Carbohydrates 27.7 g
- Sugar 2.5 g
- Protein 40.3 g
- Cholesterol 183 mg

Tasty & Crispy Chicken Tenders

Preparation Time: 10 minutes
Cooking Time: 10 minutes
Serve: 6

Ingredients:

- 2 lb chicken tenderloins
- ¼ tsp garlic powder
- ¼ tsp paprika
- 2 tsp sugar
- 1 ½ cups buttermilk
- 2 tsp salt
- For coating:
- 1 tsp baking powder
- 3 tbsp buttermilk
- 2 eggs, lightly beaten
- 2 cups flour
- ½ tsp pepper
- 1 ½ tsp salt

Directions:

1. Add chicken tenders, paprika, garlic powder, sugar, buttermilk, and salt in a zip-lock bag, seal bag, and marinate chicken tenders for 4 hours.
2. In a shallow dish, mix flour, pepper, and salt.
3. In a separate shallow dish, whisk eggs, baking powder, and buttermilk.
4. Toss chicken with flour mixture then dip in the egg mixture and again coat with flour mixture.
5. Preheat the peanut oil to 350 F in electric fryer.
6. Add coated chicken in a basket and fry in hot oil for 10 minutes or until golden brown. Drain on paper towels.
7. Serve and enjoy.

Nutritional Value (Amount per Serving):

- Calories 593
- Fat 22.7 g
- Carbohydrates 77.6 g
- Sugar 8.4 g
- Protein 18.6 g
- Cholesterol 72 mg

Ranch Chicken Tenders

Preparation Time: 10 minutes
Cooking Time: 6 minutes
Serve: 6

Ingredients:

- 2 eggs, lightly beaten
- 2 lbs chicken breasts, skinless, boneless, & sliced
- 1 oz ranch dressing mix
- 1 cup all-purpose flour

Directions:

1. In a shallow dish, mix flour and dry ranch dressing mix.
2. In a separate bowl, whisk eggs.
3. Dip each chicken piece in egg then coat with flour mixture.
4. Preheat the peanut oil to 375 F in electric fryer.
5. Add coated chicken in a basket and fry in hot oil for 6 minutes or until golden brown. Drain on paper towels.
6. Serve and enjoy.

Nutritional Value (Amount per Serving):

- Calories 386
- Fat 12.9 g
- Carbohydrates 16.3 g
- Sugar 0.3 g
- Protein 47.8 g
- Cholesterol 189 mg

Tasty Popcorn Chicken

Preparation Time: 10 minutes

Cooking Time: 5 minutes

Serve: 4

Ingredients:

- 1 ½ lbs chicken breasts, skinless, boneless, & cut into 1-inch pieces
- 2 tbsp hot sauce
- 2 cups buttermilk
- For coating:
- ½ tsp cayenne
- 1 tsp baking powder
- 1 tsp black pepper
- 2 tsp paprika
- 2 tsp onion powder
- 2 tsp garlic powder
- 1 tbsp chili powder
- 2 ½ cups all-purpose flour
- 1 tsp salt

Directions:

1. In a large bowl, whisk buttermilk and hot sauce. Add chicken pieces and mix well. Cover and place in the refrigerator for 1 hour.
2. In a mixing bowl, mix together flour and remaining coating ingredients.
3. Remove chicken pieces from the buttermilk mixture and place them into the flour mixture and toss until well coated.
4. Preheat the peanut oil to 350 F in electric fryer.
5. Add coated chicken pieces in a basket and fry in hot oil for 4-5 minutes or until golden brown. Drain on paper towels. Cook chicken pieces in batches.
6. Serve and enjoy.

Nutritional Value (Amount per Serving):

- Calories 678
- Fat 15 g
- Carbohydrates 70.3 g
- Sugar 7.2 g
- Protein 62.2 g
- Cholesterol 156 mg

Spicy Chicken Wings

Preparation Time: 10 minutes
Cooking Time: 10 minutes
Serve: 6

Ingredients:

- 12 chicken wings
- 2 cups flour
- 2 tbsp hot sauce
- 3 eggs, lightly beaten

For rub:

- ½ tsp poultry seasoning
- 1 tsp lemon pepper
- 1 tsp cayenne
- 1 tsp black pepper
- 1 tsp onion powder
- 1 tsp brown sugar
- 1 ½ tsp paprika

Directions:

1. Add chicken wings and rub ingredients into the mixing bowl and coat well. Cover bowl and place in the refrigerator for 1 hour.
2. In a shallow bowl, whisk eggs with hot sauce.
3. In a separate bowl, add flour.
4. Dip chicken wings in egg mixture then coat with flour.
5. Preheat the peanut oil to 350 F in electric fryer.
6. Add coated chicken wings in basket and fry in hot oil for 8-10 minutes or until golden brown. Drain on paper towels.
7. Serve and enjoy.

Nutritional Value (Amount per Serving):

- Calories 122
- Fat 4.8 g
- Carbohydrates 17.8 g
- Sugar 2 g
- Protein 3.5 g
- Cholesterol 0 mg

Flavorful Chicken Bites

Preparation Time: 10 minutes
Cooking Time: 10 minutes
Serve: 16

Ingredients:

- 1 rotisserie chicken, shredded
- 2 cups breadcrumbs
- 3 eggs, lightly beaten
- 1 cup all-purpose flour
- ¼ cup green onions, sliced
- 1 ¾ cups cheddar cheese, shredded
- 1 tsp pepper
- ¼ cup hot sauce

Directions:

1. In a mixing bowl, mix shredded chicken, green onions, cheese, pepper, and hot sauce.
2. Make 1-inch balls from chicken mixture and place onto the parchment-lined baking sheet and place in the refrigerator for 30 minutes.
3. In three separate bowls, add flour, eggs, and breadcrumbs.
4. Roll each chicken ball in the flour then dip in egg and coat with breadcrumbs.
5. Preheat the peanut oil to 350 F in electric fryer.
6. Add chicken balls in the basket and fry in hot oil for 2 minutes or until golden brown. Drain on paper towels. Fry chicken balls in batches.
7. Serve and enjoy.

Nutritional Value (Amount per Serving):

- Calories 145
- Fat 5.7 g
- Carbohydrates 16.2 g
- Sugar 1.1 g
- Protein 6.8 g
- Cholesterol 44 mg

Honey Garlic Butter Chicken Wings

Preparation Time: 10 minutes
Cooking Time: 12 minutes
Serve: 6

Ingredients:

- 2 lbs chicken wings
- 1 ½ tsp garlic powder
- 1 tsp baking powder
- ¼ cup self-rising flour
- 1 tsp pepper
- 1 ½ tsp salt

For sauce:

- ½ tsp garlic powder
- ¼ cup honey
- ¼ cup butter, melted

Directions:

1. In a mixing bowl, add chicken wings, garlic powder, baking powder, flour, pepper, and salt and toss well. Cover and place in the refrigerator for 30 minutes.
2. Preheat the peanut oil to 360 F in electric fryer.
3. Add chicken wings in basket and fry in hot oil for 12 minutes or until golden brown. Drain on paper towels.
4. Add chicken wings to the mixing bowl.
5. Mix garlic powder, honey, and butter and pour over chicken wings. Toss to coat.
6. Serve and enjoy.

Nutritional Value (Amount per Serving):

- Calories 422
- Fat 18.9 g
- Carbohydrates 16.9 g
- Sugar 11.9 g
- Protein 44.6 g
- Cholesterol 155 mg

Asian Chicken Fingers

Preparation Time: 10 minutes
Cooking Time: 6 minutes
Serve: 6

Ingredients:

- 2 eggs, lightly beaten
- ¼ tsp sesame seeds
- ½ cup coconut flakes
- 1 cup breadcrumbs
- ½ cup all-purpose flour
- 2 lbs chicken tenders, skinless & boneless
- Pepper
- Salt

For sauce:

- ½ tsp sesame oil
- 3 tbsp hot water
- ½ tsp red chili flakes
- ¼ tsp ground ginger
- ¼ cup soy sauce
- 1 garlic clove, minced
- 1 tbsp rice vinegar
- ¾ cup peanut butter

Directions:

1. In a shallow bowl, mix flour, ¼ tsp pepper, and ¼ tsp salt.
2. In a separate bowl, whisk eggs.
3. In a shallow dish, mix breadcrumbs, sesame seeds, coconut, ½ tsp pepper, and ½ tsp salt.
4. Coat chicken with flour then dip in egg and finally coat with breadcrumb mixture.
5. Preheat the peanut oil to 350 F in electric fryer.
6. Add coated chicken in a basket and fry in hot oil for 6 minutes or until golden brown. Drain on paper towels.
7. In a small bowl, mix together all sauce ingredients.
8. Serve chicken with sauce.

Nutritional Value (Amount per Serving):

- Calories 643
- Fat 32.6 g
- Carbohydrates 29.5 g
- Sugar 4.9 g
- Protein 58.1 g
- Cholesterol 189 mg

Fried Chicken Livers

Preparation Time: 10 minutes
Cooking Time: 5 minutes
Serve: 6

Ingredients:

- 1 lb chicken livers, trimmed
- 1 ½ tsp ground cumin
- 2 tsp pepper
- 2 tsp cayenne pepper
- 3 eggs, lightly beaten
- 3 cups all-purpose flour
- ½ cup mayonnaise
- 1 ½ tbsp soy sauce
- 1/3 cup hot sauce
- 3 ½ cups buttermilk
- 1 tsp garlic salt

Directions:

1. In a mixing bowl, whisk 2 cups buttermilk with soy sauce and hot sauce. Add chicken livers and coat well. Cover and place in the refrigerator for overnight.
2. In a shallow bowl, add 1 ½ cup flour.
3. In a separate shallow bowl, whisk eggs with remaining buttermilk.
4. In a shallow dish, mix remaining flour, cumin, pepper, cayenne, and garlic salt.
5. Remove livers from buttermilk and coat with flour then dip in the egg mixture and finally coat with seasoned flour mixture.
6. Preheat the peanut oil to 350 F in electric fryer.
7. Add coated livers in the basket and fry in hot oil for 5 minutes or until golden brown. Drain on paper towels.
8. Serve and enjoy.

Nutritional Value (Amount per Serving):

- Calories 530
- Fat 15.8 g
- Carbohydrates 61.9 g
- Sugar 8.9 g
- Protein 33.3 g
- Cholesterol 518 mg

Southern Chicken Tenders

Preparation Time: 10 minutes
Cooking Time: 6 minutes
Serve: 6

Ingredients:

- 1 egg
- 2 lbs chicken tenderloins
- 1 tsp ground turmeric
- 1 tsp dried thyme
- 1 tsp paprika
- 1 tsp pepper
- 1 tsp garlic powder
- ½ tsp ground sage
- ½ tsp onion powder
- 1 cup flour
- ½ cup buttermilk
- 1 tsp salt

Directions:

1. In a shallow bowl, whisk egg with buttermilk.
2. In a separate shallow bowl, mix flour and spices.
3. Dip chicken in egg mixture then coat with flour mixture.
4. Preheat the peanut oil to 375 F in electric fryer.
5. Add coated chicken in a basket and fry in hot oil for 6 minutes or until golden brown. Drain on paper towels.
6. Serve and enjoy.

Nutritional Value (Amount per Serving):

- Calories 278
- Fat 5.9 g
- Carbohydrates 36.1 g
- Sugar 7.8 g
- Protein 14.1 g
- Cholesterol 55 mg

Lemon Pepper Chicken Wings

Preparation Time: 10 minutes
Cooking Time: 8 minutes
Serve: 4

Ingredients:

- 12 chicken wings
- 1 tbsp lemon juice
- ½ tbsp lemon pepper seasoning
- ¼ cup butter, melted

Directions:

1. In a small bowl, add lemon juice, lemon pepper seasoning, and melted butter and mix well. Set aside.
2. Preheat the peanut oil to 350 F in electric fryer.
3. Add chicken wings in basket and fry in hot oil for 8 minutes or until golden brown. Drain on paper towels.
4. Transfer chicken wings to the mixing bowl. Pour lemon juice mixture over chicken wings and toss well.
5. Serve and enjoy.

Nutritional Value (Amount per Serving):

- Calories 581
- Fat 43.6 g
- Carbohydrates 16.7 g
- Sugar 0.1 g
- Protein 29.5 g
- Cholesterol 147 mg

Delicious Tequila Lime Chicken Wings

Preparation Time: 10 minutes

Cooking Time: 8 minutes

Serve: 4

Ingredients:

- 12 chicken wings
- ½ cup honey
- 4 tbsp orange juice
- 6 tbsp lime juice
- ¾ cup tequila
- ½ tsp salt

Directions:

1. Add tequila, honey, orange juice, lime juice, and salt in a saucepan and cook over medium heat until sauce is reduced by 2/3. Remove saucepan from heat.
2. Preheat the peanut oil to 375 F in electric fryer.
3. Add chicken wings in basket and fry in hot oil for 8 minutes or until golden brown. Drain on paper towels.
4. Transfer chicken wings in mixing bowl and toss with sauce.
5. Serve and enjoy.

Nutritional Value (Amount per Serving):

- Calories 716
- Fat 32.1 g
- Carbohydrates 52.7 g
- Sugar 36.1 g
- Protein 29.5 g
- Cholesterol 116 mg

Fried Asian Chicken Drumsticks

Preparation Time: 10 minutes
Cooking Time: 8 minutes
Serve: 3

Ingredients:

- 6 chicken drumsticks
- 3 tbsp all-purpose flour
- 1 tbsp cornstarch
- ½ tsp sesame oil
- 1 egg white
- ½ tbsp sugar
- 1 tbsp shrimp sauce

Directions:

1. In a mixing bowl, mix shrimp sauce, sugar, egg white, sesame oil, cornstarch, and flour.
2. Add chicken drumsticks into the bowl and coat well. Cover and marinate for 4 hours.
3. Preheat the peanut oil to 350 F in electric fryer.
4. Add marinated chicken drumsticks in the basket and fry in hot oil for 8 minutes or until golden brown. Drain on paper towels.
5. Serve and enjoy.

Nutritional Value (Amount per Serving):

- Calories 222
- Fat 6.1 g
- Carbohydrates 12.4 g
- Sugar 3.2 g
- Protein 27.4 g
- Cholesterol 81 mg

Fried Honey Garlic Chicken Wings

Preparation Time: 10 minutes
Cooking Time: 10 minutes
Serve: 4

Ingredients:

- 2 lbs chicken wings
- 1 cup flour
- For sauce:
- 1 ½ tbsp cornstarch
- ½ cup water
- ½ cup honey
- ¼ cup soy sauce
- 8 garlic cloves, minced
- 1/3 cup butter

Directions:

1. Melt butter in a saucepan over medium heat. Add garlic and sauté for 2 minutes.
2. Add honey and soy sauce and bring to boil. Turn heat to low and simmer for 5 minutes.
3. In a separate bowl, whisk cornstarch in water. Pour into the saucepan and whisk until well combined and continue to simmer until the sauce thickened. Remove saucepan from heat and set aside.
4. Toss chicken wings with flour.
5. Preheat the peanut oil to 350 F in electric fryer.
6. Add chicken wings in basket and fry in hot oil for 8-10 minutes or until golden brown. Drain on paper towels.
7. Transfer chicken wings in mixing bowl and toss with sauce.
8. Serve and enjoy.

Nutritional Value (Amount per Serving):

- Calories 838
- Fat 32.5 g
- Carbohydrates 64.7 g
- Sugar 35.2 g
- Protein 70.5 g
- Cholesterol 243 mg

Sriracha Chicken Wings

Preparation Time: 10 minutes
Cooking Time: 10 minutes
Serve: 4

Ingredients:

- 2 lbs chicken wings
- ½ cup honey
- 2/3 cup sriracha sauce
- 2 tbsp rice vinegar
- 4 garlic cloves, minced
- 1 onion, minced
- 2 tbsp olive oil
- 1 cup flour

Directions:

1. Heat oil in a saucepan over medium heat. Add garlic and onions and sauté until tender. Stir in honey, sriracha sauce, and vinegar and bring to boil over low heat.
2. Cook sauce for a few minutes. Remove from heat and let it cool. Pour sauce mixture into a blender and blend until smooth.
3. Toss chicken wings with flour.
4. Preheat the peanut oil to 350 F in electric fryer.
5. Add chicken wings in basket and fry in hot oil for 8-10 minutes or until golden brown. Drain on paper towels.
6. Transfer chicken wings in mixing bowl and toss with sauce.
7. Serve and enjoy.

Nutritional Value (Amount per Serving):

- Calories 754
- Fat 24.2 g
- Carbohydrates 62.3 g
- Sugar 36.1 g
- Protein 69.5 g
- Cholesterol 202 mg

Lemon Pepper Chicken

Preparation Time: 10 minutes
Cooking Time: 2 hours
Serve: 6

Ingredients:

- 3 ½ lbs whole chicken
- ½ cup lemon pepper

Directions:

1. Add ½ cup lemon pepper and 1-quart water in a large zip-lock bag. Add chicken seal bag and place in the refrigerator for 8 hours.
2. Preheat the peanut oil to 350 F in electric fryer.
3. Place marinated chicken in a basket and fry in hot oil for 2 hours or until the internal temperature of chicken reaches 165 F.
4. Slice and serve.

Nutritional Value (Amount per Serving):

- Calories 511
- Fat 19.7 g
- Carbohydrates 2.1 g
- Sugar 0 g
- Protein 76.9 g
- Cholesterol 235 mg

Fried Cornish Hen

Preparation Time: 10 minutes
Cooking Time: 14 minutes
Serve: 2

Ingredients:

- 1 whole Cornish hen, remove giblets & rinse
- 1 tsp poultry seasoning
- 1 tsp Creole seasoning

Directions:

1. Rub hen with poultry seasoning and Creole seasoning.
2. Preheat the peanut oil to 350 F in electric fryer.
3. Place hen in the basket and fry in hot oil for 14 minutes.
4. Serve and enjoy.

Nutritional Value (Amount per Serving):

- Calories 83
- Fat 4.1 g
- Carbohydrates 0.5 g
- Sugar 0 g
- Protein 10.7 g
- Cholesterol 51 mg

Flavorful Chicken Wings

Preparation Time: 10 minutes
Cooking Time: 10 minutes
Serve: 6

Ingredients:

- 3 lbs chicken wings
- 2 tbsp BBQ rub
- 2 tbsp olive oil

Directions:

1. Toss chicken wings with oil and BBQ rub.
2. Preheat the peanut oil to 375 F in electric fryer.
3. Place chicken wings in basket and fry in hot oil for 8-10 minutes.
4. Serve and enjoy.

Nutritional Value (Amount per Serving):

- Calories 471
- Fat 21.5 g
- Carbohydrates 0 g
- Sugar 0 g
- Protein 65 g
- Cholesterol 202 mg

Old Bay Chicken Wings

Preparation Time: 10 minutes
Cooking Time: 10 minutes
Serve: 6

Ingredients:

- 2 lbs chicken wings
- 2 tbsp Worcestershire sauce
- 2 tbsp hot sauce
- 2 tbsp butter, melted
- 1 tsp baking powder
- 1 tbsp old bay seasoning
- 1 tsp salt

Directions:

1. In a mixing bowl, mix old bay seasoning, baking powder, and salt. Add chicken wings into the bowl and toss well.
2. Preheat the peanut oil to 375 F in electric fryer.
3. Place chicken wings in basket and fry in hot oil for 8-10 minutes.
4. In a large bowl, mix butter, hot sauce, and Worcestershire sauce. Add chicken wings and toss well.
5. Serve and enjoy.

Nutritional Value (Amount per Serving):

- Calories 328
- Fat 15.1 g
- Carbohydrates 1.5 g
- Sugar 1.1 g
- Protein 43 g
- Cholesterol 145 mg

Cajun Chicken Wings

Preparation Time: 10 minutes

Cooking Time: 10 minutes

Serve: 4

Ingredients:

- 2 lbs chicken wings
- 2 tbsp Cajun spice rub
- 1 cup flour

Directions:

1. In a mixing bowl, toss chicken wings with Cajun spices rub, and flour.
2. Preheat the peanut oil to 350 F in electric fryer.
3. Place chicken wings in basket and fry in hot oil for 8-10 minutes.
4. Serve and enjoy.

Nutritional Value (Amount per Serving):

- Calories 672
- Fat 27.2 g
- Carbohydrates 32.4 g
- Sugar 3.5 g
- Protein 70.1 g
- Cholesterol 211 mg

Chinese Chicken Wings

Preparation Time: 10 minutes
Cooking Time: 10 minutes
Serve: 6

Ingredients:

- 24 chicken wings
- 3 tbsp honey
- 3 garlic cloves, crushed
- 1 ½ tsp ginger, grated
- ¾ cup dry sherry
- ¾ cup soy sauce

Directions:

1. Add chicken wings, honey, garlic, ginger, sherry, and soy sauce in a large mixing bowl and toss well. Cover and place in the refrigerator for overnight.
2. Preheat the peanut oil to 360 F in electric fryer.
3. Place chicken wings in basket and fry in hot oil for 8-10 minutes.
4. Serve and enjoy.

Nutritional Value (Amount per Serving):

- Calories 464
- Fat 28 g
- Carbohydrates 15 g
- Sugar 9 g
- Protein 35 g
- Cholesterol 104 mg

Shawarma Chicken Wings

Preparation Time: 10 minutes
Cooking Time: 20 minutes
Serve: 4

Ingredients:

- 1 ½ lbs chicken wings
- For marinade:
- ½ cup olive oil
- ¼ tsp cayenne
- ½ tsp pepper
- ½ tsp cinnamon
- 1 tsp turmeric
- 1 tsp paprika
- 1 tsp ground cumin
- 1 tbsp ground coriander
- 1 tsp salt

Directions:

1. Add chicken wings and marinade ingredients into the mixing bowl and mix well. Cover and place in the refrigerator for 30 minutes.
2. Preheat the peanut oil to 350 F in electric fryer.
3. Place chicken wings in basket and fry in hot oil for 8-10 minutes.
4. Serve and enjoy.

Nutritional Value (Amount per Serving):

- Calories 546
- Fat 38.1 g
- Carbohydrates 1.4 g
- Sugar 0.1 g
- Protein 49.5 g
- Cholesterol 151 mg

Chicken with Vegetables

Preparation Time: 10 minutes
Cooking Time: 25 minutes
Serve: 2

Ingredients:

- 2 chicken breasts, skinless, boneless & sliced
- ¼ lb fresh snow peas
- 2 celery stalks, sliced
- 2 carrots, peeled & sliced
- ½ lb mushrooms halved
- Pepper
- Salt

Directions:

1. Fill the inner pot with water till MAX fill line.
2. Turn the dial to 375 F. Allow water to boil for 15 minutes.
3. Add mushrooms, carrots, and celery to the basket. Season chicken with pepper and salt and place on top of vegetables. Cover and steam for 20 minutes.
4. Add snow peas on top of chicken. Cover and steam for 5 minutes more.
5. Serve and enjoy.

Nutritional Value (Amount per Serving):

- Calories 353
- Fat 11.3 g
- Carbohydrates 14.3 g
- Sugar 7.4 g
- Protein 48.3 g
- Cholesterol 130 mg

Quick & Healthy Chicken Salad

Preparation Time: 10 minutes

Cooking Time: 15 minutes

Serve: 4

Ingredients:

- 1 ¼ lbs chicken breasts, skinless & boneless
- ¼ cup raisins
- ¼ cup sunflower seeds
- ½ cup celery, diced
- 1/8 tsp pepper
- ½ tsp sea salt
- For dressing:
- ½ cup fresh chives, chopped
- 1 tbsp lemon juice
- 1 ½ tsp dried tarragon
- ¼ tsp garlic powder
- ½ tbsp Dijon mustard
- ¼ cup mayonnaise

Directions:

1. Fill the inner pot with water till MAX fill line.
2. Turn the dial to 375 F. Allow water to boil for 15 minutes.
3. Place chicken breasts in basket and boil for 15 minutes or until the internal temperature of chicken breast reaches 165 F. Drain and place in a large bowl.
4. Shred the chicken using a fork. Add raisins, sunflower seeds, celery, pepper, and salt and mix well.
5. Mix together dressing ingredients and pour over salad and stir well.
6. Serve and enjoy.

Nutritional Value (Amount per Serving):

- Calories 378
- Fat 17.1 g
- Carbohydrates 12.4 g
- Sugar 6.8 g
- Protein 42.5 g
- Cholesterol 130 mg

Poached Chicken Breast

Preparation Time: 10 minutes
Cooking Time: 20 minutes
Serve: 4

Ingredients:

- 1 lb chicken breasts, skinless & boneless
- 1 tsp Italian seasoning
- ¼ tsp pepper
- 1 tbsp salt

Directions:

1. Fill the inner pot with water till MAX fill line. Add Italian seasoning, pepper, and salt to the water.
2. Turn the dial to 375 F. Allow water to boil for 15 minutes.
3. Place chicken breasts in the basket and boil for 20 minutes or until tender. Drain and place on serving platter.
4. Serve and enjoy.

Nutritional Value (Amount per Serving):

- Calories 219
- Fat 8.8 g
- Carbohydrates 0.2 g
- Sugar 0.1 g
- Protein 32.8 g
- Cholesterol 102 mg

Boil & Broil Chicken Wings

Preparation Time: 10 minutes
Cooking Time: 25 minutes
Serve: 4

Ingredients:

- 1 lb chicken wings
- 1 tsp onion powder
- 1 tsp chili flakes
- 1 tsp garlic powder
- 1 tbsp cayenne pepper
- 1 tbsp kosher salt
- For sauce:
- 1 stick butter
- ½ cup hot sauce

Directions:

1. Fill the inner pot with water till MAX fill line. Add spices and salt to the water.
2. Turn the dial to 375 F. Allow water to boil for 15 minutes.
3. Place chicken wings in basket and boil for 15 minutes or until tender. Drain and place on the baking sheet.
4. Broil chicken wings for 10 minutes.
5. Melt butter in a pan over medium heat. Add hot sauce and stir well and cook for 2 minutes.
6. Add chicken wings into the large mixing bowl. Pour sauce over chicken wings and toss well.
7. Serve and enjoy.

Nutritional Value (Amount per Serving):

- Calories 430
- Fat 31.7 g
- Carbohydrates 2.3 g
- Sugar 0.9 g
- Protein 33.6 g
- Cholesterol 162 mg

Tasty Chicken Salad

Preparation Time: 10 minutes
Cooking Time: 30 minutes
Serve: 6

Ingredients:

- 3 chicken breasts, boneless
- ¼ cup sweet pickle relish
- 1 tbsp dill
- 1 tbsp vinegar
- 1 tbsp sugar
- 1 cup miracle whip
- 1 cup mayonnaise
- 3 celery stalks, diced
- Pepper
- Salt

Directions:

1. Fill the inner pot with water till MAX fill line.
2. Turn the dial to 375 F. Allow water to boil for 15 minutes.
3. Place chicken breasts in the basket and boil for 30 minutes or until tender. Drain and place in a large bowl.
4. Shred the chicken using a fork. Add remaining ingredients and mix well.
5. Serve and enjoy.

Nutritional Value (Amount per Serving):

- Calories 445
- Fat 31.8 g
- Carbohydrates 18.8 g
- Sugar 9.3 g
- Protein 22 g
- Cholesterol 89 mg

Healthy Shredded Chicken

Preparation Time: 10 minutes
Cooking Time: 15 minutes
Serve: 2

Ingredients:

- 2 chicken breasts, skinless & boneless
- Pepper
- Salt

Directions:

1. Fill the inner pot with water till MAX fill line.
2. Turn the dial to 375 F. Allow water to boil for 15 minutes.
3. Place chicken breasts in the basket and boil for 15 minutes or until tender. Drain and place in a large bowl.
4. Shred the chicken using a fork.
5. Season with pepper and salt.
6. Serve and enjoy.

Nutritional Value (Amount per Serving):

- Calories 278
- Fat 10.8 g
- Carbohydrates 0 g
- Sugar 0 g
- Protein 42.3 g
- Cholesterol 130 mg

Chapter 3: Pork, Beef & Lamb

Crispy Pork Chops

Preparation Time: 10 minutes
Cooking Time: 10 minutes
Serve: 4

Ingredients:

- 4 pork chops, boneless
- 2 cups buttermilk
- 1 tsp pepper
- 1 tsp salt
- For coating:
- 1 ½ cups flour
- 1 tsp garlic powder
- 1 tsp onion powder
- 1 tsp pepper
- 2 tsp paprika
- ½ cup cornstarch
- 2 tsp salt

Directions:

1. In a bowl, mix buttermilk, pepper, and salt. Add pork chops and coat well. Cover and place in the refrigerator for 6 hours.
2. In a shallow dish, mix coating ingredients.
3. Remove pork chops from buttermilk and coat with flour mixture.
4. Preheat the peanut oil to 350 F in electric fryer.
5. Add pork chops to the basket and fry in hot oil for 10 minutes or until the internal temperature of pork chops reaches to 145 F.
6. Serve and enjoy.

Nutritional Value (Amount per Serving):

- Calories 547
- Fat 21.6 g
- Carbohydrates 58.5 g
- Sugar 6.5 g
- Protein 27.4 g
- Cholesterol 74 mg

Southern Pork Chops

Preparation Time: 10 minutes
Cooking Time: 10 minutes
Serve: 4

Ingredients:

- 4 pork chops
- 1 tsp pepper
- 2 tbsp butter
- 1 cup flour
- 1 tsp garlic salt

Directions:

1. In a shallow dish, mix flour, pepper, and garlic salt.
2. Brush pork chops with butter and coat with flour mixture.
3. Preheat the peanut oil to 350 F in electric fryer.
4. Add pork chops in the basket and fry in hot oil for 10 minutes or until internal temperature reaches to 145 F.
5. Serve and enjoy.

Nutritional Value (Amount per Serving):

- Calories 424
- Fat 26 g
- Carbohydrates 24.7 g
- Sugar 0.3 g
- Protein 21 g
- Cholesterol 84 mg

Easy Boston Butt

Preparation Time: 10 minutes
Cooking Time: 3 hours 30 minutes
Serve: 12

Ingredients:

- 8 lb pork butt
- 4 tbsp Cajun spice
- 6 tbsp yellow mustard

Directions:

1. Season pork butt with Cajun spice and mustard.
2. Preheat the peanut oil to 325 F in electric fryer.
3. Add pork butt in the basket and fry in hot oil for 3 ½ hours or until internal temperature reaches to 160 F.
4. Serve and enjoy.

Nutritional Value (Amount per Serving):

- Calories 589
- Fat 20.5 g
- Carbohydrates 0.4 g
- Sugar 0.1 g
- Protein 94.5 g
- Cholesterol 278 mg

Honey Mustard Ham

Preparation Time: 10 minutes

Cooking Time: 25 minutes

Serve: 12

Ingredients:

- 10 lbs ham
- 1 tbsp Dijon mustard
- ¼ cup brown sugar
- ¼ cup honey

Directions:

1. Mix together honey, Brown sugar, and Dijon mustard and rub over ham.
2. Preheat the peanut oil to 350 F in electric fryer.
3. Add ham in basket and fry in hot oil for 25 minutes or until the internal temperature of ham reaches to 140 F.
4. Serve and enjoy.

Nutritional Value (Amount per Serving):

- Calories 650
- Fat 32 g
- Carbohydrates 23 g
- Sugar 8 g
- Protein 62 g
- Cholesterol 215 mg

Baby Back Ribs

Preparation Time: 10 minutes
Cooking Time: 9 minutes
Serve: 6

Ingredients:

- 2 racks baby back ribs
- 1 tsp poultry seasoning

Directions:

1. Season baby back ribs with poultry seasoning.
2. Preheat the peanut oil to 375 F in electric fryer.
3. Add baby back ribs in the basket and fry in hot oil for 9 minutes or until internal temperature reaches to 140 F.
4. Serve and enjoy.

Nutritional Value (Amount per Serving):

- Calories 672
- Fat 53.4 g
- Carbohydrates 8 g
- Sugar 0 g
- Protein 36 g
- Cholesterol 183 mg

Asian Pork

Preparation Time: 10 minutes
Cooking Time: 4 minutes
Serve: 4

Ingredients:

- 1 lb pork tenderloin, sliced
- 1 ½ cup breadcrumbs
- ½ cup flour
- 1 tsp cornstarch
- 1 ½ tbsp oyster sauce
- 1 tbsp Shaoxing wine
- 2 tbsp soy sauce
- ½ tsp white pepper
- 4 eggs, lightly beaten

Directions:

1. In a mixing bowl, add meat, cornstarch, oyster sauce, wine, soy sauce, and white pepper and mix well. Cover and marinate for 30 minutes.
2. In a shallow dish, add flour.
3. In a separate shallow dish, whisk eggs.
4. In a shallow bowl, add breadcrumbs.
5. Coat marinated meat with flour then dip in egg and finally coat with breadcrumbs.
6. Preheat the peanut oil to 350 F in electric fryer.
7. Place coated meat in a basket and fry in hot oil for 4 minutes.
8. Serve and enjoy.

Nutritional Value (Amount per Serving):

- Calories 450
- Fat 10 g
- Carbohydrates 43 g
- Sugar 3 g
- Protein 42 g
- Cholesterol 246 mg

Mexican Pork Chops

Preparation Time: 10 minutes
Cooking Time: 6 minutes
Serve: 4

Ingredients:

- 4 pork chops
- 1 tsp cumin
- 2 tsp chili powder
- 1 tbsp brown sugar
- 2 tbsp olive oil
- Pepper
- Salt

Directions:

1. Add pork chops and remaining ingredients into the mixing bowl and coat well. Cover and marinate for 15 minutes.
2. Preheat the peanut oil to 350 F in electric fryer.
3. Add pork chops in the basket and fry in hot oil for 4 minutes or until internal temperature reaches to 145 F.
4. Serve and enjoy.

Nutritional Value (Amount per Serving):

- Calories 331
- Fat 27 g
- Carbohydrates 3 g
- Sugar 2 g
- Protein 18 g
- Cholesterol 69 mg

Fried Pork Ribs

Preparation Time: 10 minutes
Cooking Time: 6 minutes
Serve: 4

Ingredients:

- 1 lb pork ribs, cut into bite size pieces
- 2 tbsp potato starch
- 1 tsp sesame oil
- Pepper
- Salt

Directions:

1. Add meat pieces and remaining ingredients into the mixing bowl and toss well.
2. Preheat the peanut oil to 350 F in electric fryer.
3. Add meat pieces in a basket and fry in hot oil until golden brown.
4. Serve and enjoy.

Nutritional Value (Amount per Serving):

- Calories 320
- Fat 21.2 g
- Carbohydrates 0 g
- Sugar 0 g
- Protein 30 g
- Cholesterol 117 mg

Pork Nuggets

Preparation Time: 10 minutes
Cooking Time: 13 minutes
Serve: 4

Ingredients:

- 1 egg
- 1 tbsp cayenne
- 2 tbsp paprika
- 2 cups flour
- 1 ½ cups buttermilk
- 2 lbs pork loin, cut into chunks
- 1 ½ cups whole grain mustard
- ¼ cup vinegar
- 1 tbsp garlic, minced
- ¼ cup pickled jalapenos, minced
- 1 tbsp chives, chopped

Directions:

1. In a mixing bowl, add meat chunks, chives, jalapenos, garlic, vinegar, and mustard and mix well. Cover and marinate for 30 minutes.
2. In a shallow bowl, mix flour, paprika, and cayenne.
3. In a separate bowl, mix buttermilk and egg.
4. Add marinated meat chunks in buttermilk mixture then coat with flour mixture.
5. Preheat the peanut oil to 375 F in electric fryer.
6. Add meat pieces in a basket and fry in hot oil for 4 minutes. Cook in batches.
7. Serve and enjoy.

Nutritional Value (Amount per Serving):

- Calories 910
- Fat 37g
- Carbohydrates 61 g
- Sugar 5 g
- Protein 73 g
- Cholesterol 226 mg

Fried Pork Steak

Preparation Time: 10 minutes
Cooking Time: 30 minutes
Serve: 12

Ingredients:

- 4 lbs pork steaks
- 1 tsp paprika
- 1 tsp turmeric
- 1 tsp cumin
- 1 tsp dried basil
- 1 tsp coriander
- 1 tsp cinnamon
- 1 tsp chili powder
- 4 tbsp garlic salt
- 2 tbsp garlic powder
- 2 cups flour
- 1 tbsp salt

Directions:

1. Add steaks and remaining ingredients into the large zip-lock bag. Seal bag and coat well.
2. Preheat the peanut oil to 375 F in electric fryer.
3. Add coated steaks in the basket and fry in hot oil until golden brown. Cook in batches.
4. Serve and enjoy.

Nutritional Value (Amount per Serving):

- Calories 484
- Fat 25 g
- Carbohydrates 19 g
- Sugar 1 g
- Protein 41 g
- Cholesterol 144 mg

Fried Pork Belly

Preparation Time: 10 minutes
Cooking Time: 16 minutes
Serve: 6

Ingredients:

- 2 lbs pork belly
- 5 garlic cloves, crushed
- 1 tbsp soy sauce
- 2 tsp peppercorn
- 3 tbsp salt
- 4 cups water

Directions:

1. Add pork belly, garlic, soy sauce, peppercorn, salt, and water in large pot and cook until pork belly is tender.
2. Drain pork belly well and cut into pieces.
3. Preheat the peanut oil to 375 F in electric fryer.
4. Add pork belly pieces in a basket and fry in hot oil for 5 minutes or until golden brown. Cook in batches.
5. Serve and enjoy.

Nutritional Value (Amount per Serving):

- Calories 507
- Fat 29 g
- Carbohydrates 35 g
- Sugar 18.2 g
- Protein 26.7 g
- Cholesterol 103 mg

Fried Pork Ribs

Preparation Time: 10 minutes

Cooking Time: 15 minutes

Serve: 6

Ingredients:

- 2 lbs pork ribs, cut into chunks
- For marinade:
- 1 tbsp cornflour
- 3 tbsp flour
- 1 egg
- ½ tsp five-spice powder
- 1 tsp sesame oil
- 1 tbsp oyster sauce
- 1 tbsp sugar
- 1 tbsp Shaoxing wine
- 1 tbsp ginger juice

Directions:

1. Add meat chunks and marinade ingredients into the zip-lock bag. Seal bag and shake well and let it marinate for 2 hours.
2. Preheat the peanut oil to 350 F in electric fryer.
3. Add marinated meat pieces in a basket and fry in hot oil until golden brown. Cook in batches.
4. Serve and enjoy.

Nutritional Value (Amount per Serving):

- Calories 460
- Fat 28 g
- Carbohydrates 6 g
- Sugar 2 g
- Protein 41 g
- Cholesterol 183 mg

Steak Bites

Preparation Time: 10 minutes
Cooking Time: 25 minutes
Serve: 8

Ingredients:

- 1 egg
- 2 lbs steak, cut into chunks
- ¼ tsp cayenne
- ½ tsp garlic powder
- 1 tsp pepper
- 2 tsp dry mesquite seasoning
- 2 cups flour
- ¼ cup milk
- 1 tsp salt

Directions:

1. In a shallow bowl, whisk egg and milk.
2. In a separate bowl, mix flour, seasoning, pepper, garlic powder, cayenne, and salt.
3. Dip meat pieces in egg mixture then coat with flour mixture.
4. Preheat the peanut oil to 365 F in electric fryer.
5. Add coated meat pieces in a basket and fry in hot oil for 5 minutes. Cook in batches.
6. Serve and enjoy.

Nutritional Value (Amount per Serving):

- Calories 353
- Fat 6.7 g
- Carbohydrates 24 g
- Sugar 0.5 g
- Protein 45 g
- Cholesterol 123 mg

Chili Beef

Preparation Time: 10 minutes
Cooking Time: 22 minutes
Serve: 2

Ingredients:

- ½ lb beef flank, cut into strips
- ½ tsp pepper
- 1 egg, lightly beaten
- 1 tsp chili flakes
- 1 ½ tsp five-spice powder
- 2 ½ tbsp cornstarch
- 1 tsp sea salt

Directions:

1. Toss meat strips with pepper, egg, chili flakes, spice powder, cornstarch, and salt.
2. Preheat the peanut oil to 350 F in electric fryer.
3. Add coated meat strips in the basket and fry in hot oil for 2 minutes or until golden brown. Cook in batches.
4. Serve and enjoy.

Nutritional Value (Amount per Serving):

- Calories 291
- Fat 11 g
- Carbohydrates 9.7 g
- Sugar 0.2 g
- Protein 34 g
- Cholesterol 144 mg

Simple Fried Steaks

Preparation Time: 10 minutes
Cooking Time: 5 minutes
Serve: 2

Ingredients:

- 2 sirloin steaks
- 1 tsp Montreal steak seasoning

Directions:

1. Season steaks with seasoning.
2. Preheat the peanut oil to 350 F in electric fryer.
3. Add steaks in the basket and fry in hot oil for 4-5 minutes.
4. Serve and enjoy.

Nutritional Value (Amount per Serving):

- Calories 111
- Fat 4 g
- Carbohydrates 0.5 g
- Sugar 0 g
- Protein 18 g
- Cholesterol 0 mg

Meatballs

Preparation Time: 10 minutes
Cooking Time: 20 minutes
Serve: 4

Ingredients:

- 1 lb ground beef
- 1 tbsp sugar
- ½ tsp chili flakes
- 1 tsp all-purpose flour
- 2 green onions, chopped
- 1 tbsp cilantro, chopped
- 2 tsp sesame oil
- 1 tbsp soy sauce
- 1 egg white
- ¼ tsp pepper
- ½ tsp salt

Directions:

1. Fill inner pot with water till MAX fill line.
2. Turn dial to 375 F. Allow water to boil for 15 minutes.
3. Add all ingredients into the mixing bowl and mix until well combined. Make balls from meat mixture.
4. Place meatballs in the basket. Cover and steam for 20 minutes.
5. Serve and enjoy.

Nutritional Value (Amount per Serving):

- Calories 254
- Fat 9.4 g
- Carbohydrates 4.5 g
- Sugar 3.3 g
- Protein 35.8 g
- Cholesterol 101 mg

Chapter 4: Fish & Seafood

Coconut Shrimp

Preparation Time: 10 minutes
Cooking Time: 5 minutes
Serve: 4

Ingredients:

- 15 oz shrimp, peeled
- 2 egg whites
- 1/4 tsp cayenne pepper
- 1/2 cup shredded coconut
- 1/2 cup breadcrumbs
- 1/2 tsp salt

Directions:

1. Whisk egg whites in a shallow dish.
2. In a bowl, mix together shredded coconut, breadcrumbs, and cayenne pepper.
3. Dip shrimp into the egg mixture then coat with coconut mixture.
4. Preheat the peanut oil to 350 F in electric fryer.
5. Add shrimp in the basket and fry in hot oil for 4-5 minutes.
6. Serve and enjoy.

Nutritional Value (Amount per Serving):

- Calories 224
- Fat 5.9 g
- Carbohydrates 13 g
- Sugar 1.6 g
- Protein 28.2 g
- Cholesterol 224 mg

Fried Calamari

Preparation Time: 10 minutes
Cooking Time: 5 minutes
Serve: 3

Ingredients:

- 12 oz squid, cleaned & cut into ½-inch ring
- 1/8 tsp cayenne pepper
- 2 oz cornstarch
- 4 oz flour
- 1 egg, lightly beaten
- 1/8 tsp salt

Directions:

1. Add squid and egg in a large bowl and mix well.
2. In a separate bowl, mix flour, cornstarch, cayenne, and salt.
3. Coat squid ring with flour mixture.
4. Preheat the peanut oil to 350 F in electric fryer.
5. Add squid in the basket and fry in hot oil until golden brown.
6. Serve and enjoy.

Nutritional Value (Amount per Serving):

- Calories 335
- Fat 3.4 g
- Carbohydrates 49.8 g
- Sugar 0.2 g
- Protein 23.5 g
- Cholesterol 319 mg

Shrimp Balls

Preparation Time: 10 minutes
Cooking Time: 5 minutes
Serve: 4

Ingredients:

- 8 oz shrimp, peeled, deveined, & minced
- 12 bread slices, crumbled
- 2 tsp potato starch
- 1 tsp sugar
- ½ tsp salt

Directions:

1. Add all ingredients into the mixing bowl and mix until well combined.
2. Make balls from mixture and place into the basket.
3. Preheat the peanut oil to 320 F in electric fryer.
4. Add shrimp balls in the basket and fry in hot oil until golden brown.
5. Serve and enjoy.

Nutritional Value (Amount per Serving):

- Calories 143
- Fat 1.9 g
- Carbohydrates 15.5 g
- Sugar 2.2 g
- Protein 15 g
- Cholesterol 119 mg

Southern Shrimp

Preparation Time: 10 minutes

Cooking Time: 2 minutes

Serve: 4

Ingredients:

- 1 lb shrimp, peeled & deveined
- 1 ½ tbsp old bay seasoning
- 2 cups flour
- 1 cup buttermilk

Directions:

1. In a small bowl, add buttermilk.
2. In a separate shallow dish, mix flour and old bay seasoning.
3. Dip shrimp in buttermilk then coat with flour mixture.
4. Preheat the peanut oil to 350 F in electric fryer.
5. Add shrimp to the basket and fry in hot oil for 2 minutes or until golden brown.
6. Serve and enjoy.

Nutritional Value (Amount per Serving):

- Calories 387
- Fat 3.1 g
- Carbohydrates 52.3 g
- Sugar 3.1 g
- Protein 34.3 g
- Cholesterol 241 mg

Fried Salmon

Preparation Time: 10 minutes
Cooking Time: 12 minutes
Serve: 4

Ingredients:

- 4 salmon fillets
- ½ cup water
- 1 tbsp Cajun seasoning
- 1 cup flour
- Pepper
- Salt

Directions:

1. In a shallow bowl, mix flour, Cajun seasoning, pepper, salt, and water.
2. Add fish fillets in flour mixture and coat well.
3. Preheat the peanut oil to 350 F in electric fryer.
4. Add coated fish fillets in the basket and fry in hot oil for 12 minutes or until golden brown.
5. Serve and enjoy.

Nutritional Value (Amount per Serving):

- Calories 351
- Fat 11.3 g
- Carbohydrates 24.1 g
- Sugar 0.3 g
- Protein 37.8 g
- Cholesterol 78 mg

Fried Catfish Fillets

Preparation Time: 10 minutes
Cooking Time: 25 minutes
Serve: 8

Ingredients:

- 1 lb catfish fillets
- 2 tsp hot sauce
- 2 eggs, lightly beaten
- ¼ tsp paprika
- ½ tsp lemon pepper
- ½ tsp cayenne pepper
- ½ tsp black pepper
- 1 ½ tsp garlic salt
- ¼ cup flour
- 2/3 cup cornmeal

Directions:

1. In a shallow bowl, whisk eggs with hot sauce.
2. In a separate shallow dish, mix flour, cornmeal, pepper, cayenne pepper, lemon pepper, paprika, and salt.
3. Dip fish fillet in egg then coat with flour mixture.
4. Preheat the peanut oil to 350 F in electric fryer.
5. Add coated fish fillets in the basket and fry in hot oil until golden brown.
6. Serve and enjoy.

Nutritional Value (Amount per Serving):

- Calories 146
- Fat 5.8 g
- Carbohydrates 11.6 g
- Sugar 0.3 g
- Protein 11.6 g
- Cholesterol 68 mg

Spicy Fish Nuggets

Preparation Time: 10 minutes
Cooking Time: 10 minutes
Serve: 6

Ingredients:

- 1 lb white fish fillet, boneless & cut into cubes
- 1 egg
- 2 tbsp milk
- 2 tbsp dried parsley
- ¼ cup flour
- ¾ cup breadcrumbs

Directions:

1. In a shallow bowl, whisk egg with milk.
2. In a shallow dish, mix breadcrumbs, parsley, and flour.
3. Dip fish cubes in egg then coat with breadcrumb mixture.
4. Preheat the peanut oil to 350 F in electric fryer.
5. Add coated fish pieces in a basket and fry in hot oil until golden brown.
6. Serve and enjoy.

Nutritional Value (Amount per Serving):

- Calories 216
- Fat 7.3 g
- Carbohydrates 14 g
- Sugar 1.2 g
- Protein 22 g
- Cholesterol 86 mg

Garlic Butter Fish Fillet

Preparation Time: 10 minutes
Cooking Time: 10 minutes
Serve: 3

Ingredients:

- 12 oz white fish fillets, cut into pieces
- 2 tbsp olive oil
- 2 tbsp cornstarch
- 1/8 tsp cayenne
- Pepper
- Salt
- For sauce:
- 1 tbsp parsley, chopped
- ½ tbsp lemon juice
- 3 garlic clove, minced
- ½ stick butter, melted

Directions:

1. In a mixing bowl, add fish pieces, oil, cornstarch, cayenne, pepper, and salt. Toss well.
2. Preheat the peanut oil to 350 F in electric fryer.
3. Add coated fish pieces in a basket and fry in hot oil until golden brown.
4. In a large bowl, mix butter, garlic, lemon juice, and parsley. Add fried fish and toss well.
5. Serve and enjoy.

Nutritional Value (Amount per Serving):

- Calories 436
- Fat 33.2 g
- Carbohydrates 6 g
- Sugar 0.1 g
- Protein 28.2 g
- Cholesterol 128 mg

Parmesan Shrimp

Preparation Time: 10 minutes
Cooking Time: 5 minutes
Serve: 4

Ingredients:

- 1 lb shrimp, deveined and cleaned
- 1 tbsp lemon juice
- 1/4 cup salad dressing
- 1 oz parmesan cheese, grated
- 1 tbsp garlic, minced

Directions:

1. Fill inner pot with water till MAX fill line.
2. Turn dial to 375 F. Allow water to boil for 15 minutes.
3. Place shrimp in a basket. Cover and steam for 4-5 minutes.
4. Meanwhile, for the sauce in a bowl, mix together the remaining ingredients.
5. Add shrimp in a sauce bowl and toss well.
6. Transfer shrimp into the bowl. Add remaining ingredients over shrimp and stir well.
7. Serve and enjoy.

Nutritional Value (Amount per Serving):

- Calories 220
- Fat 8.4 g
- Carbohydrates 6.3 g
- Sugar 1 g
- Protein 28.4 g
- Cholesterol 248 mg

Herb Salmon

Preparation Time: 10 minutes
Cooking Time: 10 minutes
Serve: 2

Ingredients:

- 2 salmon fillets
- 1 tsp garlic, minced
- 1 tbsp thyme, diced
- 1 tbsp parsley, diced
- 2 tsp lime zest
- 2 tsp lemon zest
- 1 tbsp olive oil
- Pepper
- Salt

Directions:

1. In a small bowl, mix together lime zest, lemon zest, oil, garlic, thyme, parsley, pepper, and salt and rub over salmon.
2. Fill inner pot with water till MAX fill line.
3. Turn dial to 375 F. Allow water to boil for 15 minutes.
4. Place salmon in the basket. Cover and steam for 10 minutes.
5. Serve and enjoy.

Nutritional Value (Amount per Serving):

- Calories 305
- Fat 18.1 g
- Carbohydrates 2.2 g
- Sugar 0.2 g
- Protein 34.9 g
- Cholesterol 78 mg

Salmon Croquettes

Preparation Time: 10 minutes
Cooking Time: 7 minutes
Serve: 4

Ingredients:

- 2 eggs, beaten
- 1 lb can red salmon, drained and mashed
- 1 cup breadcrumbs
- 1/3 cup olive oil

Directions:

1. In a bowl, add drained salmon, eggs, and parsley. Mix well.
2. In a shallow dish, combine together breadcrumbs and oil.
3. Make 16 croquettes from the salmon mixture and coat with breadcrumbs.
4. Preheat the peanut oil to 350 F in electric fryer.
5. Add croquettes in the basket and fry in hot oil for 7 minutes or until golden brown.
6. Serve and enjoy.

Nutritional Value (Amount per Serving):

- Calories 363
- Fat 27 g
- Carbohydrates 6 g
- Sugar 1 g
- Protein 24 g
- Cholesterol 129 mg

Country Shrimp Boil

Preparation Time: 10 minutes

Cooking Time: 15 minutes

Serve: 4

Ingredients:

- 1 lb shrimp, peel
- ½ lb sausage, sliced
- 1 lb corn on the cob, cut into pieces
- 1 lb baby potatoes, cut in half
- ¼ cup butter, melted

Directions:

1. Fill inner pot with water till MAX fill line.
2. Turn dial to 375 F. Allow water to boil for 15 minutes.
3. Place potatoes in basket and boil for 12 minutes.
4. Add shrimp, sausage, and corn and cook for 3 minutes.
5. Pour melted butter over shrimp mixture and serve.

Nutritional Value (Amount per Serving):

- Calories 600
- Fat 30.5 g
- Carbohydrates 41.2 g
- Sugar 4.1 g
- Protein 43.4 g
- Cholesterol 317 mg

Salmon Patties

Preparation Time: 10 minutes
Cooking Time: 10 minutes
Serve: 8

Ingredients:

- 14 oz can salmon, drained
- ½ tsp pepper
- 1 tsp lemon juice
- 2 eggs, lightly beaten
- ½ onion, chopped
- ½ tsp salt

Directions:

1. Add all ingredients into the mixing bowl and mix until well combined.
2. Make patties from mixture.
3. Preheat the peanut oil to 350 F in electric fryer.
4. Add patties in the basket and fry in hot oil for 5 minutes on each side or until golden brown.
5. Serve and enjoy.

Nutritional Value (Amount per Serving):

- Calories 101
- Fat 4.7 g
- Carbohydrates 0.8 g
- Sugar 0.4 g
- Protein 13.1 g
- Cholesterol 63 mg

Tasty Fish Balls

Preparation Time: 10 minutes
Cooking Time: 5 minutes
Serve: 6

Ingredients:

- 8 oz cooked fish, remove bones
- 1 egg, lightly beaten
- 1 lb potato, mashed
- Pepper
- Salt

Directions:

1. Add all ingredients into the mixing bowl and mix until well combined.
2. Make balls from mixture.
3. Preheat the peanut oil to 350 F in electric fryer.
4. Add balls in the basket and fry in hot oil until golden brown.
5. Serve and enjoy.

Nutritional Value (Amount per Serving):

- Calories 180
- Fat 6 g
- Carbohydrates 13 g
- Sugar 0.7 g
- Protein 7 g
- Cholesterol 27 mg

Delicious Fried Fish

Preparation Time: 10 minutes
Cooking Time: 10 minutes
Serve: 4

Ingredients:

- 1 lb fish fillets
- 1 tsp ginger garlic paste
- 1/8 tsp mustard
- Pepper
- Salt

Directions:

1. Coat fish fillets with ginger garlic paste and mustard and season with pepper and salt.
2. Preheat the peanut oil to 350 F in electric fryer.
3. Add fish fillets in the basket and fry in hot oil until golden brown from both the sides.
4. Serve and enjoy.

Nutritional Value (Amount per Serving):

- Calories 264
- Fat 14 g
- Carbohydrates 19 g
- Sugar 0 g
- Protein 16 g
- Cholesterol 39 mg

Crab Balls

Preparation Time: 10 minutes
Cooking Time: 5 minutes
Serve: 6

Ingredients:

- 1 egg
- 1 lb crabmeat
- 1 tsp dry mustard
- 1 tsp Worcestershire sauce
- ½ tsp old bay seasoning
- ¼ cup mayonnaise
- ½ cup breadcrumbs
- 1 /4 tsp pepper
- ¼ tsp salt

Directions:

1. Add all ingredients into the mixing bowl and mix until well combined.
2. Make balls from mixture.
3. Preheat the peanut oil to 350 F in electric fryer.
4. Add balls in the basket and fry in hot oil and cook for 4-5 minutes or until golden brown.
5. Serve and enjoy.

Nutritional Value (Amount per Serving):

- Calories 160
- Fat 5 g
- Carbohydrates 20 g
- Sugar 6 g
- Protein 8 g
- Cholesterol 45 mg

Asian Shrimp

Preparation Time: 10 minutes
Cooking Time: 5 minutes
Serve: 4

Ingredients:

- 1 lb shrimp, peeled and deveined
- 1/4 tsp ginger, minced
- 2 garlic cloves, minced
- 2 tbsp soy sauce
- 2 tbsp chili sauce

Directions:

1. Fill inner pot with water till MAX fill line.
2. Turn dial to 375 F. Allow water to boil for 15 minutes.
3. Place shrimp in basket. Cover and steam for 4-5 minutes.
4. Meanwhile, for the sauce in a bowl, mix together the remaining ingredients.
5. Add shrimp in a sauce bowl and toss well.
6. Serve and enjoy.

Nutritional Value (Amount per Serving):

- Calories 150
- Fat 2 g
- Carbohydrates 5 g
- Sugar 0.3 g
- Protein 26.5 g
- Cholesterol 239 mg

Quick Old Bay Shrimp

Preparation Time: 10 minutes

Cooking Time: 6 minutes

Serve: 2

Ingredients:

- 1/2 lb shrimp, peeled and deveined
- 3/4 tsp cayenne pepper
- 1 tbsp olive oil
- 1/2 tsp old bay seasoning
- 1/4 tsp paprika
- 1/8 tsp salt

Directions:

1. Add all ingredients into the mixing bowl and toss well.
2. Fill inner pot with water till MAX fill line.
3. Turn dial to 375 F. Allow water to boil for 15 minutes.
4. Place shrimp in basket. Cover and steam for 6 minutes.
5. Serve and enjoy.

Nutritional Value (Amount per Serving):

- Calories 195
- Fat 9.1 g
- Carbohydrates 2.3 g
- Sugar 0.1 g
- Protein 26 g
- Cholesterol 239 mg

Easy Sriracha Salmon

Preparation Time: 10 minutes
Cooking Time: 12 minutes
Serve: 2

Ingredients:

- 2 salmon fillets, skin on
- 1 tbsp soy sauce
- 3 tbsp sriracha
- 6 tbsp honey

Directions:

1. In a bowl, mix together soy sauce, sriracha, and honey. Add salmon fillets to the bowl and coat well and let it sit for 30 minutes.
2. Fill inner pot with water till MAX fill line.
3. Turn dial to 375 F. Allow water to boil for 15 minutes.
4. Place salmon in basket. Cover and steam for 10-12 minutes.
5. Serve and enjoy.

Nutritional Value (Amount per Serving):

- Calories 455
- Fat 11 g
- Carbohydrates 57 g
- Sugar 51.9 g
- Protein 35.2 g
- Cholesterol 78 mg

Shrimp Fajitas

Preparation Time: 10 minutes
Cooking Time: 12 minutes
Serve: 6

Ingredients:

- 1/2 lb shrimp
- 1/2 green bell pepper, diced
- 1/2 red bell pepper, diced
- 1 tbsp taco seasoning
- 1/4 cup onion, diced
- Pepper
- Salt

Directions:

1. Add all ingredients into the bowl and toss well.
2. Fill inner pot with water till MAX fill line.
3. Turn dial to 375 F. Allow water to boil for 15 minutes.
4. Add shrimp mixture in the basket. Cover and steam for 10-12 minutes.
5. Serve and enjoy.

Nutritional Value (Amount per Serving):

- Calories 55
- Fat 0.8 g
- Carbohydrates 2.5 g
- Sugar 1 g
- Protein 9 g
- Cholesterol 80 mg

Steam Garlic Prawns

Preparation Time: 10 minutes
Cooking Time: 12 minutes
Serve: 2

Ingredients:

- 8 prawns
- 2 tbsp olive oil
- 4 garlic cloves, minced

Directions:

1. Fill inner pot with water till MAX fill line.
2. Turn dial to 375 F. Allow water to boil for 15 minutes.
3. Add prawns in basket. Cover and steam for 10 minutes.
4. Heat oil in a pan over medium heat. Add garlic and sauté for 2 minutes.
5. Pour oil garlic mixture over prawns.
6. Serve and enjoy.

Nutritional Value (Amount per Serving):

- Calories 234
- Fat 15 g
- Carbohydrates 3 g
- Sugar 0.1 g
- Protein 20.4 g
- Cholesterol 185 mg

Steam Cod

Preparation Time: 10 minutes
Cooking Time: 10 minutes
Serve: 4

Ingredients:

- 4 cod fillets
- 2 tbsp Dijon mustard
- 1 tbsp lemon juice
- 1 tbsp parsley, chopped
- 1 tbsp tarragon, chopped
- 1 tbsp dill, chopped
- 1 tbsp cilantro, chopped
- ¼ tsp pepper
- ¼ tsp salt

Directions:

1. In a small bowl, mix mustard, lemon juice, parsley, tarragon, dill, cilantro, pepper, and salt. Set aside.
2. Fill inner pot with water till MAX fill line.
3. Turn dial to 375 F. Allow water to boil for 15 minutes.
4. Place cod fillets in basket. Cover and steam for 5 minutes.
5. Spread mustard paste on top of cod fillets. Cover and steam for 5 minutes more.
6. Serve and enjoy.

Nutritional Value (Amount per Serving):

- Calories 90
- Fat 0.6 g
- Carbohydrates 1.3 g
- Sugar 0.2 g
- Protein 19.7 g
- Cholesterol 80 mg

Steam Salmon

Preparation Time: 10 minutes
Cooking Time: 10 minutes
Serve: 4

Ingredients:

- 4 salmon fillets, skinless & boneless
- ½ tsp red pepper, crushed
- ¼ cup honey
- ¼ cup soy sauce
- 1 tsp garlic powder
- 2 tsp ground ginger
- ¼ tsp pepper
- ½ tsp kosher salt

Directions:

1. Season salmon fillets with garlic powder, pepper, and salt.
2. Fill inner pot with water till MAX fill line.
3. Turn dial to 375 F. Allow water to boil for 15 minutes.
4. Place salmon fillets in basket. Cover and steam for 8-10 minutes.
5. Add honey, soy sauce, red pepper, and ginger in a saucepan and cook for 2-3 minutes.
6. Pour sauce over salmon and serve.

Nutritional Value (Amount per Serving):

- Calories 319
- Fat 11 g
- Carbohydrates 21 g
- Sugar 18 g
- Protein 36 g
- Cholesterol 78 mg

Steam Scallops

Preparation Time: 10 minutes
Cooking Time: 8 minutes
Serve: 2

Ingredients:

- 8 scallops
- ½ tsp garlic, minced
- ½ tsp dried basil

Directions:

1. Fill inner pot with water till MAX fill line.
2. Turn dial to 375 F. Allow water to boil for 15 minutes.
3. Toss scallops with garlic and basil.
4. Add scallops in basket. Cover and steam for 8 minutes.
5. Serve and enjoy.

Nutritional Value (Amount per Serving):

- Calories 107
- Fat 0.9 g
- Carbohydrates 3 g
- Sugar 0 g
- Protein 20 g
- Cholesterol 40 mg

Boil White Fish Fillets

Preparation Time: 10 minutes
Cooking Time: 10 minutes
Serve: 4

Ingredients:

- 1 ½ lbs frozen white fish fillets
- ¼ tsp garlic powder
- ½ stick butter, melted

Directions:

1. Fill inner pot with water till MAX fill line. Add old bay seasoning in the water.
2. Turn dial to 375 F. Allow water to boil for 15 minutes.
3. Add white fish fillets in basket and boil for 10 minutes. Drain well and transfer on a platter.
4. Season fish fillets with garlic powder. Pour melted butter over fish fillets.
5. Serve and enjoy.

Nutritional Value (Amount per Serving):

- Calories 245
- Fat 12 g
- Carbohydrates 0.1 g
- Sugar 0.1 g
- Protein 34.9 g
- Cholesterol 30 mg

Quick & Boiled Shrimp

Preparation Time: 10 minutes

Cooking Time: 3 minutes

Serve: 4

Ingredients:

- 1 lbs shrimp
- Pepper
- Salt

Directions:

1. Fill inner pot with water till MAX fill line. Add old bay seasoning in the water.
2. Turn dial to 375 F. Allow water to boil for 15 minutes.
3. Add shrimp in basket and boil for 3 minutes. Season with pepper and salt.
4. Serve and enjoy.

Nutritional Value (Amount per Serving):

- Calories 135
- Fat 1.9 g
- Carbohydrates 1.7 g
- Sugar 0 g
- Protein 25.8 g
- Cholesterol 239 mg

Steam Lobster

Preparation Time: 10 minutes
Cooking Time: 15 minutes
Serve: 4

Ingredients:

- 2 lbs lobsters
- 2 tbsp butter, melted
- Salt

Directions:

1. Fill inner pot with water till MAX fill line. Add old bay seasoning in the water.
2. Turn dial to 375 F. Allow water to boil for 15 minutes.
3. Add lobsters in basket. Cover and steam for 15 minutes.
4. Pour melted butter over lobsters and season with salt.
5. Serve and enjoy.

Nutritional Value (Amount per Serving):

- Calories 254
- Fat 7.6 g
- Carbohydrates 0 g
- Sugar 0 g
- Protein 43.2 g
- Cholesterol 346 mg

Steam Clams

Preparation Time: 10 minutes

Cooking Time: 5 minutes

Serve: 4

Ingredients:

- 2 lbs clams
- 3 lemon slices
- 2 garlic cloves, minced
- 2 tbsp butter, melted

Directions:

1. Fill inner pot with water till MAX fill line. Add old bay seasoning in the water.
2. Turn dial to 375 F. Allow water to boil for 15 minutes.
3. Add clams in basket. Cover and steam for 3 minutes.
4. Melt butter in a pan over medium heat.
5. Add garlic and sauté for 2 minutes.
6. Pour butter garlic mixture over clams. Add lemon slices and toss well.
7. Serve and enjoy.

Nutritional Value (Amount per Serving):

- Calories 164
- Fat 6.2 g
- Carbohydrates 25.8 g
- Sugar 7.7 g
- Protein 1.6 g
- Cholesterol 15 mg

Easy Crab Legs

Preparation Time: 10 minutes
Cooking Time: 8 minutes
Serve: 4

Ingredients:

- 4 clusters snow crab legs
- ½ cup butter, melted

Directions:

1. Fill inner pot with water till MAX fill line. Add old bay seasoning in the water.
2. Turn dial to 375 F. Allow water to boil for 15 minutes.
3. Add crab legs in basket. Cover and steam for 8 minutes.
4. Pour melted butter over crab legs and serve.

Nutritional Value (Amount per Serving):

- Calories 415
- Fat 1 g
- Carbohydrates 4 g
- Sugar 1 g
- Protein 1 g
- Cholesterol 61 mg

Classic Shrimp Boil

Preparation Time: 10 minutes
Cooking Time: 20 minutes
Serve: 6

Ingredients:

- 2 lbs shrimp, peeled & deveined
- 3 tbsp butter, melted
- 1 lb smoked sausage, cut into 1-inch pieces
- 4 ears corn on the cob, cut into 4-inch pieces
- 1 lb baby potatoes, halved
- 1 onion, peeled & cut into 6 pieces
- 6 garlic cloves
- ½ cup old bay seasoning
- 3 lemons, cut into wedges

Directions:

1. Fill inner pot with water till MAX fill line. Add old bay seasoning in the water.
2. Turn dial to 375 F. Allow water to boil for 15 minutes.
3. Add potatoes, onion, and garlic in basket and boil for 10 minutes or until tender. Add sausage and corn over potatoes and cook for 4 minutes. Add shrimp and cook for 2-3 minutes.
4. Drain well and transfer in mixing bowl.
5. Add melted butter and lemon and mix well.
6. Serve and enjoy.

Nutritional Value (Amount per Serving):

- Calories 328
- Fat 28.3 g
- Carbohydrates 0 g
- Sugar 0 g
- Protein 18 g
- Cholesterol 69 mg

Chapter 5: Vegetarian

Perfect Boil Corn on the Cob

Preparation Time: 10 minutes
Cooking Time: 8 minutes
Serve: 8

Ingredients:

- 8 ears corn on the cob, remove husk & silks
- 8 tsp butter
- ¼ tsp salt

Directions:

1. Fill inner pot with water till MAX fill line.
2. Turn dial to 375 F. Allow water to boil for 15 minutes.
3. Add corn on the cobs in basket and boil for 5-8 minutes.
4. Place corn on the cob on a serving platter and serve with butter and salt.

Nutritional Value (Amount per Serving):

- Calories 92
- Fat 4.3 g
- Carbohydrates 14.1 g
- Sugar 2.3 g
- Protein 2 g
- Cholesterol 10 mg

Potato Green Bean Salad

Preparation Time: 10 minutes
Cooking Time: 22 minutes
Serve: 6

Ingredients:

- 24 oz baby potatoes
- ½ lb fresh green beans, ends trimmed
- 1 tbsp fresh chives, chopped
- 1 garlic clove, minced
- 1 tsp Dijon mustard
- 3 tbsp balsamic vinegar
- ¼ tsp pepper
- 1 tsp kosher salt

Directions:

1. Fill inner pot with water till MAX fill line.
2. Turn dial to 375 F. Allow water to boil for 15 minutes.
3. Add green beans in basket and boil for 1-2 minutes. Drain and place in large bowl.
4. Add potatoes in basket and boil for 15-20 minutes. Drain well, cut in half and place in large bowl with green beans.
5. In a small bowl, mix together vinegar, mustard, garlic, pepper, and salt and pour over green beans and potatoes.
6. Garnish with fresh chives and serve.

Nutritional Value (Amount per Serving):

- Calories 81
- Fat 0.2 g
- Carbohydrates 17.2 g
- Sugar 0.6 g
- Protein 3.7 g
- Cholesterol 0 mg

Herb Garlic Boiled Potatoes

Preparation Time: 10 minutes
Cooking Time: 20 minutes
Serve: 6

Ingredients:

- 2 lbs Yukon gold potatoes, peeled & halved
- ¼ cup olive oil
- 2 oz fresh parsley, chopped
- 2 tsp rosemary
- 3 garlic cloves, minced
- Pepper
- Salt

Directions:

1. Fill inner pot with water till MAX fill line.
2. Turn dial to 375 F. Allow water to boil for 15 minutes.
3. Add potatoes in basket and boil for 20 minutes or until potatoes are tender. Drain and place in large bowl.
4. Add parsley, rosemary, garlic, oil, pepper, and salt over potatoes and mix well.
5. Serve and enjoy.

Nutritional Value (Amount per Serving):

- Calories 122
- Fat 8.6 g
- Carbohydrates 11.5 g
- Sugar 0.5 g
- Protein 1.6 g
- Cholesterol 0 mg

Healthy Boiled Broccoli

Preparation Time: 10 minutes
Cooking Time: 5 minutes
Serve: 4

Ingredients:

- 1 lb broccoli, cut into florets
- 1 lemon, cut into wedges
- Pepper
- Salt

Directions:

1. Fill inner pot with water till MAX fill line.
2. Turn dial to 375 F. Allow water to boil for 15 minutes.
3. Add broccoli florets in basket and boil for 3-5 minutes or until broccoli are tender. Drain and place in large bowl.
4. Add lemon, pepper, and salt in broccoli and toss well.
5. Serve and enjoy.

Nutritional Value (Amount per Serving):

- Calories 39
- Fat 0.4 g
- Carbohydrates 7.6 g
- Sugar 1.9 g
- Protein 3.2 g
- Cholesterol 0 mg

Delicious Cauliflower Salad

Preparation Time: 10 minutes
Cooking Time: 8 minutes
Serve: 8

Ingredients:

- 1 cauliflower head, cut into florets
- ½ cup celery, chopped
- ½ cup radishes, sliced
- 1/3 cup dill pickles, chopped
- 2 green onions, sliced

For dressing:

- ½ tsp garlic powder
- ½ tsp black pepper
- 1 tbsp yellow mustard
- 1 cup mayonnaise
- ½ tsp salt

Directions:

1. Fill inner pot with water till MAX fill line.
2. Turn dial to 375 F. Allow water to boil for 15 minutes.
3. Add cauliflower florets in basket and boil for 8 minutes or until cauliflower are tender. Drain and place in large bowl.
4. Add celery, radishes, dill pickles, and green onion into the bowl and mix well.
5. In a small bowl, mix all dressing ingredients and pour over cauliflower mixture.
6. Mix well and serve.

Nutritional Value (Amount per Serving):

- Calories 129
- Fat 10 g
- Carbohydrates 10 g
- Sugar 3.1 g
- Protein 1.2 g
- Cholesterol 8 mg

Cauliflower Apple Salad

Preparation Time: 10 minutes
Cooking Time: 8 minutes
Serve: 6

Ingredients:

- 1 cauliflower head, cut into florets
- 1/3 cup blue cheese dressing
- 2 scallions, sliced
- 1 cup celery, sliced
- 1 large apple, diced
- Pepper
- Salt

Directions:

1. Fill inner pot with water till MAX fill line.
2. Turn dial to 375 F. Allow water to boil for 15 minutes.
3. Add cauliflower florets in basket and boil for 8 minutes or until cauliflower are tender. Drain and place in large bowl.
4. Add scallions, celery, apple, pepper, and salt and mix well.
5. Pour blue cheese dressing over salad and toss well.
6. Serve and enjoy.

Nutritional Value (Amount per Serving):

- Calories 103
- Fat 7.3 g
- Carbohydrates 9.4 g
- Sugar 5.7 g
- Protein 1.8 g
- Cholesterol 2 mg

Maple Butter Carrots

Preparation Time: 10 minutes
Cooking Time: 15 minutes
Serve: 4

Ingredients:

- 5 large carrots, peeled and chopped into rounds
- 2 tbsp butter, melted
- 1 tbsp maple syrup

Directions:

1. Fill inner pot with water till MAX fill line.
2. Turn dial to 375 F. Allow water to boil for 15 minutes.
3. Add carrots in basket and boil for 15-20 minutes or until carrots are tender. Drain and place in large bowl.
4. Pour butter and maple syrup over carrots and toss well.
5. Serve and enjoy.

Nutritional Value (Amount per Serving):

- Calories 101
- Fat 5.8 g
- Carbohydrates 12.2 g
- Sugar 7.4 g
- Protein 0.8 g
- Cholesterol 15 mg

Steamed Vegetables with Garlic

Preparation Time: 10 minutes
Cooking Time: 10 minutes
Serve: 4

Ingredients:

- 2 cups baby carrots
- 2 cups broccoli florets
- ¼ cup olive oil
- 4 garlic cloves, minced
- ½ tsp salt

Directions:

1. Fill inner pot with water till MAX fill line.
2. Turn dial to 375 F. Allow water to boil for 15 minutes.
3. Add baby carrots and broccoli florets in basket. Cover and steam for 10 minutes or until vegetables are tender. Transfer vegetables in large bowl.
4. Heat oil in a pan over medium heat.
5. Add garlic to the pan and sauté for 1-2 minutes.
6. Pour oil garlic mixture over vegetables and mix well.
7. Season with salt and serve.

Nutritional Value (Amount per Serving):

- Calories 163
- Fat 12.8 g
- Carbohydrates 12 g
- Sugar 5.8 g
- Protein 1.5 g
- Cholesterol 0 mg

Steamed Brussels Sprouts

Preparation Time: 10 minutes
Cooking Time: 6 minutes
Serve: 4

Ingredients:

- 1 lb Brussels sprouts, clean & cut in half
- 1 tbsp butter, melted
- Pepper
- Salt

Directions:

1. Fill inner pot with water till MAX fill line.
2. Turn dial to 375 F. Allow water to boil for 15 minutes.
3. Add Brussels sprouts in basket. Cover and steam for 6 minutes. Transfer Brussels sprouts in large bowl.
4. Add butter, pepper, and salt and toss well.
5. Serve and enjoy.

Nutritional Value (Amount per Serving):

- Calories 75
- Fat 3.3 g
- Carbohydrates 10.3 g
- Sugar 2.5 g
- Protein 3.9 g
- Cholesterol 8 mg

Basil Lemon Broccoli

Preparation Time: 10 minutes

Cooking Time: 10 minutes

Serve: 4

Ingredients:

- 4 cups broccoli florets
- ¼ tsp lemon juice
- ½ tsp dried basil
- 3 tbsp butter, melted

Directions:

1. Fill inner pot with water till MAX fill line.
2. Turn dial to 375 F. Allow water to boil for 15 minutes.
3. Add broccoli florets in basket. Cover and steam for 10 minutes. Transfer broccoli florets in large bowl.
4. Add butter, basil, and lemon juice toss well.
5. Serve and enjoy.

Nutritional Value (Amount per Serving):

- Calories 107
- Fat 8.9 g
- Carbohydrates 6.1 g
- Sugar 1.6 g
- Protein 2.6 g
- Cholesterol 23 mg

Steam Lemon Herb Cauliflower

Preparation Time: 10 minutes
Cooking Time: 10 minutes
Serve: 4

Ingredients:

- 1 small cauliflower head, cut into florets
- 1 tsp lemon zest
- 1/8 tsp garlic powder
- 1 tsp Italian seasoning
- 2 tbsp olive oil
- ¾ tsp kosher salt

Directions:

1. Fill inner pot with water till MAX fill line.
2. Turn dial to 375 F. Allow water to boil for 15 minutes.
3. Add cauliflower florets in basket. Cover and steam for 10 minutes. Transfer cauliflower florets in large bowl.
4. Add lemon zest, garlic powder, Italian seasoning, oil, and kosher salt over cauliflower florets and toss well.
5. Serve and enjoy.

Nutritional Value (Amount per Serving):

- Calories 81
- Fat 7.4 g
- Carbohydrates 3.8 g
- Sugar 1.7 g
- Protein 1.3 g
- Cholesterol 1 mg

Lemon Butter Baby Potatoes

Preparation Time: 10 minutes
Cooking Time: 20 minutes
Serve: 6

Ingredients:

- 1 ½ lbs baby potatoes, cut in half
- ¼ cup fresh chives, diced
- ¼ cup fresh parsley, diced
- 1 lemon juice
- 6 garlic cloves, diced
- ¼ cup butter
- Pepper
- Salt

Directions:

1. Fill inner pot with water till MAX fill line.
2. Turn dial to 375 F. Allow water to boil for 15 minutes.
3. Add potatoes in basket and boil for 20 minutes or until potatoes are tender. Drain and place in large bowl.
4. Melt butter in a pan over medium heat.
5. Add garlic and sauté until lightly browned. Add chives, parsley, half lemon juice, pepper, and salt. Stir for 1 minute and remove pan from heat.
6. Pour butter mixture and remaining lemon juice over potatoes and mix well.
7. Serve and enjoy.

Nutritional Value (Amount per Serving):

- Calories 140
- Fat 7.8 g
- Carbohydrates 15.4 g
- Sugar 0.1 g
- Protein 3.3 g
- Cholesterol 20 mg

Chapter 6: Side Dishes

Easy Pasta Salad

Preparation Time: 10 minutes
Cooking Time: 5 minutes
Serve: 10

Ingredients:

- 12 oz rotini pasta
- ½ cup Italian salad dressing
- ¼ cup onion, diced
- 2.25 oz can olives, drained
- 1 cup feta cheese, crumbled
- 1 cup cherry tomatoes, halved
- 1 cucumber, chopped
- Pepper
- Salt

Directions:

1. Fill inner pot with water till MAX fill line.
2. Turn dial to 375 F. Allow water to boil for 15 minutes.
3. Add pasta in basket and boil until al dente. Drain and place in large bowl.
4. Add remaining ingredients into the large bowl and mix well.
5. Serve and enjoy.

Nutritional Value (Amount per Serving):

- Calories 181
- Fat 7.4 g
- Carbohydrates 22.5 g
- Sugar 2.7 g
- Protein 6.4 g
- Cholesterol 46 mg

Garlic Broccoli Pasta

Preparation Time: 10 minutes
Cooking Time: 15 minutes
Serve: 4

Ingredients:

- ½ head broccoli, cut into florets
- 12 oz shell pasta
- 4 garlic cloves, minced
- ¼ cup olive oil
- ¼ tsp pepper
- ½ tsp salt

Directions:

1. Fill inner pot with water till MAX fill line.
2. Turn dial to 375 F. Allow water to boil for 15 minutes.
3. Add pasta in basket and boil until al dente. Drain and place in large bowl.
4. Add broccoli florets into the basket and boil for 7 minutes. Drain well and place in large bowl with pasta.
5. Heat oil in a pan over medium heat.
6. Add garlic and sauté for 2 minutes.
7. Pour oil garlic mixture over pasta and broccoli.
8. Season with pepper and salt.
9. Serve and enjoy.

Nutritional Value (Amount per Serving):

- Calories 358
- Fat 14.6 g
- Carbohydrates 47.6 g
- Sugar 0 g
- Protein 9.8 g
- Cholesterol 62 mg

Southern Summer Squash

Preparation Time: 10 minutes
Cooking Time: 10 minutes
Serve: 4

Ingredients:

- 3 medium summer squash, cut into ¼-inch slices
- 2 tbsp butter, melted
- 1 small onion, sliced
- Pepper
- Salt

Directions:

1. Fill inner pot with water till MAX fill line.
2. Turn dial to 375 F. Allow water to boil for 15 minutes.
3. Add squash and onion in the basket and boil until tender. Drain and place in large bowl.
4. Add butter, pepper, and salt over squash and onion and mix well.
5. Serve and enjoy.

Nutritional Value (Amount per Serving):

- Calories 66
- Fat 5.9 g
- Carbohydrates 3.3 g
- Sugar 1.8 g
- Protein 0.8 g
- Cholesterol 15 mg

Healthy Boiled Cabbage

Preparation Time: 10 minutes
Cooking Time: 8 minutes
Serve: 8

Ingredients:

- 1 small cabbage head, cut in half then cut into 1 ½-inch wedges
- 2 tbsp butter, melted
- Pepper
- Salt

Directions:

1. Fill inner pot with water till MAX fill line.
2. Turn dial to 375 F. Allow water to boil for 15 minutes.
3. Place cabbage pieces in a basket and boil for 8 minutes. Drain and place on serving platter.
4. Pour butter over cabbage wedges. Season with pepper and salt.
5. Serve and enjoy.

Nutritional Value (Amount per Serving):

- Calories 48
- Fat 3 g
- Carbohydrates 5.2 g
- Sugar 2.9 g
- Protein 1.2 g
- Cholesterol 8 mg

Steam Asparagus

Preparation Time: 10 minutes
Cooking Time: 5 minutes
Serve: 2

Ingredients:

- 1 lb asparagus, end trimmed
- 2 tbsp butter, melted
- Pepper
- Salt

Directions:

1. Fill inner pot with water till MAX fill line.
2. Turn dial to 375 F. Allow water to boil for 15 minutes.
3. Add asparagus in the basket. Cover and steam for 3-5 minutes. Transfer asparagus on serving platter.
4. Drizzle with butter and season with pepper and salt.
5. Serve and enjoy.

Nutritional Value (Amount per Serving):

- Calories 147
- Fat 11.8 g
- Carbohydrates 8.8 g
- Sugar 4.3 g
- Protein 5.1 g
- Cholesterol 31 mg

Steam Ginger Garlic Vegetables

Preparation Time: 10 minutes
Cooking Time: 7 minutes
Serve: 4

Ingredients:

- 1 large cauliflower head, cut into florets
- 2 green onions, chopped
- 2 cups sugar snap peas
- 1 red bell pepper, sliced

For dressing:

- ¼ tsp Chinese 5 spice
- ¼ tsp white pepper
- ½ tsp red chili flakes
- 1 tbsp ginger, minced
- 2 garlic cloves, minced
- 1 tbsp rice vinegar
- ¼ cup olive oil
- ½ tsp salt

Directions:

1. Fill inner pot with water till MAX fill line.
2. Turn dial to 375 F. Allow water to boil for 15 minutes.
3. Add cauliflower florets in the basket. Cover and steam for 5 minutes.
4. Add onions, pepper, and sugar snap peas over cauliflower florets and steam for 2 minutes more. Transfer vegetables in a large mixing bowl.
5. Mix together dressing ingredients and pour over steam vegetables and toss well.
6. Serve and enjoy.

Nutritional Value (Amount per Serving):

- Calories 195
- Fat 13.1 g
- Carbohydrates 17.9 g
- Sugar 8 g
- Protein 5.7 g
- Cholesterol 0 mg

Boiled Beets

Preparation Time: 10 minutes
Cooking Time: 35 minutes
Serve: 4

Ingredients:

- 1 lb beets, peel & cut into 1-inch pieces

Directions:

1. Fill inner pot with water till MAX fill line.
2. Turn dial to 375 F. Allow water to boil for 15 minutes.
3. Add beets in the basket and boil for 35 minutes.
4. Serve and enjoy.

Nutritional Value (Amount per Serving):

- Calories 122
- Fat 4.8 g
- Carbohydrates 17.8 g
- Sugar 2 g
- Protein 3.5 g
- Cholesterol 0 mg

Boil Sweet Potatoes

Preparation Time: 10 minutes
Cooking Time: 15 minutes
Serve: 6

Ingredients:

- 2 lbs sweet potatoes, peel & cut into 1-inch pieces
- Salt

Directions:

1. Fill inner pot with water till MAX fill line.
2. Turn dial to 375 F. Allow water to boil for 15 minutes.
3. Add sweet potatoes to basket and boil for 15 minutes.
4. Serve and enjoy.

Nutritional Value (Amount per Serving):

- Calories 178
- Fat 0.3 g
- Carbohydrates 42.2 g
- Sugar 0.8 g
- Protein 2.3 g
- Cholesterol 0 mg

Boiled Peanuts

Preparation Time: 10 minutes

Cooking Time: 4 hours

Serve: 6

Ingredients:

- 3 lbs raw peanuts, soak for overnight
- ¼ cup salt

Directions:

1. Fill inner pot with water till MAX fill line.
2. Turn dial to 375 F. Allow water to boil for 20 minutes. Add salt in boiling water.
3. Turn dial to 250 F.
4. Add peanuts in the basket and boil for 4 hours.
5. Serve and enjoy.

Nutritional Value (Amount per Serving):

- Calories 432
- Fat 37.8 g
- Carbohydrates 13.5 g
- Sugar 2.7 g
- Protein 18.9 g
- Cholesterol 0 mg

Healthy Steamed Veggies

Preparation Time: 10 minutes
Cooking Time: 8 minutes
Serve: 6

Ingredients:

- 2 cups cauliflower florets
- 2 cups broccoli florets
- 2 tbsp olive oil
- 2 onions, sliced
- 2 lbs squash, cubed
- 6 carrots, sliced
- 2 lbs potatoes, cut into ¼-inch slices
- ½ tsp black pepper
- ½ tsp salt

Directions:

1. Fill inner pot with water till MAX fill line.
2. Turn dial to 375 F. Allow water to boil for 15 minutes.
3. Add cauliflower florets, broccoli florets, onions, squash, carrots, and potatoes in basket. Cover and steam for 8 minutes. Transfer veggies in large mixing bowl.
4. Pour olive oil over vegetables and season with pepper and salt.
5. Serve and enjoy.

Nutritional Value (Amount per Serving):

- Calories 227
- Fat 5.3 g
- Carbohydrates 42.1 g
- Sugar 10.2 g
- Protein 6.8 g
- Cholesterol 0 mg

Steam Sugar Snap Peas

Preparation Time: 10 minutes
Cooking Time: 5 minutes
Serve: 4

Ingredients:

- 1 lb sugar snap peas
- 1 tsp black sesame seeds
- 1 ½ tsp sesame oil
- Salt

Directions:

1. Fill inner pot with water till MAX fill line.
2. Turn dial to 375 F. Allow water to boil for 15 minutes.
3. Add sugar snap peas in the basket. Cover and steam for 5 minutes. Transfer sugar snap peas to large bowl.
4. Add sesame seeds, sesame oil, and salt over sugar snap peas and mix well.
5. Serve and enjoy.

Nutritional Value (Amount per Serving):

- Calories 67
- Fat 2.3 g
- Carbohydrates 8.7 g
- Sugar 4.5 g
- Protein 3.3 g
- Cholesterol 0 mg

Fried Corn on the Cob

Preparation Time: 10 minutes
Cooking Time: 4 minutes
Serve: 6

Ingredients:

- 3 frozen corn on the cob, Cut in half & thawed
- 1 lemon juice
- Salt

Directions:

1. Preheat the peanut oil to 375 F in electric fryer.
2. Add corn on the cob in the basket and fry in hot oil for 4 minutes. Drain on paper towels.
3. Brush corn on the cob with lemon juice and season with salt.
4. Serve and enjoy.

Nutritional Value (Amount per Serving):

- Calories 30
- Fat 0 g
- Carbohydrates 6.5 g
- Sugar 1 g
- Protein 1 g
- Cholesterol 0 mg

Conclusion

The Masterbuilt electric turkey fryer is made up of stainless-steel body and comes with detachable heating elements and a control panel. It is one of the versatile cooking appliances used as a fryer, steamer, or boiler. Its large cooking basket is capable to hold up to 20 lb of turkey at a time. The fryer comes with various features like overheat protection, adjustable temperature setting knob, non-stick interior, built-in drain valve for easy cleaning, and more.

The book contains 100 different types of recipes like poultry, pork, beef & lamb, fish& seafood, vegetarian and side dishes. All the recipes written in this cookbook are unique and written in an easily understandable form. The recipes are written with their perfect preparation and cooking time with step by step cooking instructions. Finally, all the recipes end with their nutritional information.

CPSIA information can be obtained
at www.ICGtesting.com
Printed in the USA
LVHW101101181220
674416LV00007B/433

9 781954 091313